THE THEORY
AND AESTHETIC EVALUATION
OF LITERATURE

THE THEORY
AND AESTHETIC
EVALUATION
OF LITERATURE

Sister Mary Francis Slattery

Selinsgrove: Susquehanna University Press
London and Toronto: Associated University Presses

Associated University Presses
440 Forsgate Drive
Cranbury, NJ 08512

Associated University Presses
25 Sicilian Avenue
London WC1A 2QH, England

Associated University Presses
P.O. Box 488, Port Credit
Mississauga, Ontario
Canada L5G 4M2

The paper used in this publication meets the requirements
of the American National Standard for Permanence of Paper
for Printed Library Materials Z39.48-1984.

Library of Congress Cataloging-in-Publication Data

Slattery, Mary Francis, 1909–
    The theory and aesthetic evaluation of literature / Sister Mary
Francis Slattery.
        p.   cm.
    Bibliography: p
    Includes index.
    ISBN 0-945636-08-3 (alk. paper)
    1. Literature—History and criticism—Theory, etc.   2. Literature—
Aesthetics.   I. Title.
PN441.S56   1989
801'.95—dc20   88-43272
                                                                    CIP

PRINTED IN THE UNITED STATES OF AMERICA

To
students,
professors,
or
simply
perceptive
lovers
of
literature

Contents

Introduction

THIS book is directed to students in advanced degree programs studying the literature of any language, and possibly to young professors who might be seeking to clarify the differences between the tradition and a recent departure from it. The thrust is primarily, although not exhaustively, theoretical; and the concepts are in agreement with the tradition that I perceive to be long and illustrious.

At the present time, in quite a few classrooms, the study of "English" has changed beyond recognition. Books are still visible, but students and even professors are becoming less and less sure about what is to be done with them. If not lured outright to the "new directions" taken by deconstructionists, they are at least puzzled. What is needed for any informed choice whatsoever is knowledge of the value of each tenet of the new theories.

Some questions currently confronting serious readers about literature are the same as those that have been asked and variously answered for centuries. But additional, more radical questions have recently been challenging students and teachers; now, the *existence* of literature seems to be threatened. After all, what is it, and of *essentially* what value is it? My emphasis is on the word *essentially* in the question, since a genuine literary work can have several values.

The theory of literature is a system of general concepts constituting knowledge of what literature is. It originates in close scrutiny of literary works and is enriched and corrected by historical study of the theory of literature up to the present. Knowing the history is a safeguard against repeating old theoretical errors. What is sought in this study is accuracy of literary theory. The witty inscription on the Archives Building in Washington, D.C., suggests that acquaintance with history safeguards right judgment about anything. On the other hand, Jacques Derrida, the patriarch of deconstruction, interprets Rousseau as saying that "reading should free itself . . . from . . . history," in his preface to *Of Grammatology*.[1] Meanwhile, although it is not the focus of this study, I have adverted to history when relevant.

The same is true with regard to value. Evaluation—that is, the demonstration of value—presupposes knowledge of what value is, and awareness of the history of such knowledge safeguards its accuracy.

Thus, since I direct my inquiry principally to the nature of value as such and then to that of specific values in literature, I also occasionally invoke the history of both of these.

Significant contemporary opposition to the views expressed here, especially that of deconstructionists, I shall occasionally identify in passing. The deconstructionist trend does not seem to be primarily literary, but exists rather in the larger area of philosophy, particularly metaphysics, although this is not a universally voiced opinion.

Deconstructionism is traceable as one of two radically distinct views of reality. One, thought to have originated with Heraclitus, and to have been espoused by Plato, sees all reality as *process;* the other, that of Aristotle, sees reality as *both process and product.* Although the long history of philosophy includes a multiplicity of innovations, that same root difference is still recognizable in this decade.

The theory and evaluation of literature advanced here will show adherence to the idea of including both process and product.

After briefly indicating the common confusion of literature with rhetoric, I mean to explore the theories of literature and that of value, the nature of aesthetic value indispensable to literature and its dependence upon hazard, and, finally, the particular aesthetic values that qualify traditional literature.

For readers who prefer to be shown, this study will conclude with the demonstration of aesthetic values of specific works. Because some features on which the aesthetic essentially depends can be microscopic, the scrutiny in the last section may occasionally be detailed and, as such, not important to an experienced reader. If not indispensable, they are nevertheless included for readers to whom they may prove helpful.

Finally, because the progress of the text will alternate between sections borrowing from history and therefore heavily footnoted on the one hand, and other sections that are theoretical and relatively free of notes on the other, some readers may do well enough to ignore signals to notes. They are included mainly as guides to detours for student research, if desired.

THE THEORY
AND AESTHETIC EVALUATION
OF LITERATURE

1

Preliminary Distinctions: Rhetoric and Poetic

THE natural speech process is observable among persons from babyhood to advanced age, educated or illiterate. Human beings are social, and as such they communicate with one another. Although a great variety of reasons could be found to motivate such utterances, these are alike in that they are not programmed. They are spontaneous and natural, simply communicative. In being spontaneous and natural they differ from rhetorical and poetic utterances, which are "artistic."

It seems useful to mention a few ideas about rhetoric, because (1) like literature, which is the focus of this study, it is an art that uses language as its material, and therefore, as experience has shown, it can be confused with literature, which here will be called poetry; and (2) literature, although it is not rhetoric, has rhetorical aspects, another reason for the confusion sometimes experienced.

As long ago as the fifth century B.C., political leaders in Athens and the Greek Islands and provinces of the empire programmed speech in order to arouse in their listeners determination to action. Even in the epics of Homer, which were composed considerably earlier, the heroes made speeches that caused their listeners to change their minds, and these persuasive speeches later became models of technique for students of the *art* of rhetoric, or, as we more commonly say, oratory.[1]

The art seems to have flourished in the Greek colony of Sicily and was later brought to Athens, where it was viewed with alarm,[2] seeming to some Athenians to be persuasion at all costs, even the cost of truth. The experts were *sophists,* whose moral purpose was characteristically deficient in responsibility.[3]

Rhetoric had flare-ups of popularity throughout early and late antiquity, and had both direct and collateral descendants in the Middle Ages and the Renaissance[4] as well as in modern times. Our present concern is that it must be viewed for what it is in itself and thus not confused with the art of poetry. The theory of poetry (the word *poetry* used here in the broad sense to include epic, tragedy, comedy, lyric, the novel, and the short story) is our subject.

The "art of rhetoric" is the "faculty of observing in any given case the available means of persuasion."[5] The art is not persuasion, the speech is; the art is the *faculty of observing the means* of persuading. And the subject matter is whatever might be suitable in a given case, so persuasion as such has no definite subject matter. The rational control of every kind of interaction (subtle, natural process) between a speaker and an addressee in order somehow to affect and persuade the latter is the art exercised by the orator.

Statesmen in ancient Greece and especially in Rome went to schools of rhetoric where they gradually mastered the art.[6] In recent times this classical rhetoric has been traceable in speeches of an occasional sophisticated statesman, the study having been retained in a few places. The most reliable concept of rhetoric is Aristotle's, that its purpose is to have an effect on an addressee.[7]

Poetry is radically distinct from rhetoric. Poetic speech, like that of rhetoric, deviates from the normal speech process.[8] However, its fundamental difference from rhetoric resides in the fact that the primary end or purpose of poetry is not in the addressee.

True, as Craig La Drière pointed out, the distinction between them is not always an absolute one, each sometimes having properties of the other. The usefulness of the distinction between them will be "impaired if the forms of discourse be conceived as mutually exclusive categories. . . . Probably no discourse can be purely rhetorical or purely poetic."[9]

At this stage, three main ideas expressed about the poetic process have emerged: (1) poetry is speech; (2) like rhetoric, it deviates from the normal speech process; but (3) it is distinct from rhetoric.

It is speech. That in modern times most of our literature comes to us from our reading the printed page rather than from hearing vocal utterance blurs our awareness that poetry is speech. The truth remains, though; the print is merely a means of representing to us words that are (or could be or might have been) spoken.[10] Even a lyric, for instance, shaped in solitude with no vocal sound uttered, is still imagined speech. Speech is an instrument of a social being for expressing consciousness, and if a poet shapes a lyric poem in a way that expresses *a* consciousness,

even should he be *imagining* a person (who might or might not
exist in reality) having the precise consciousness thus uniquely
expressed, the lyric is imagined speech, detached from the reality of one person talking to another.[11]

If it does not express a consciousness of a person existing in
reality, why call it speech then? Modern linguists, at least since
the time of Ferdinand de Saussure, have recognized both speech
and grammar as belonging to language. Grammar *(langue)* is a
system of norms to which speech *(parole)* may or may not conform. *Langue* comprises the logical conventions that constitute
the unity of *language*. *Parole* is individual speech, imagined or
spoken or written.

Spoken language is carried by sound waves to the eardrum,
which vibrates. The vibrations are carried thence by the auditory
nerve to the brain, where the composition of vibrations is registered as an *acoustic image*. Instantly a meaning conventionally
attached to that image is registered—a mentioned thing, place,
person, relationship, or concept with which the acoustic image is
habitually associated. The locus of the association between the
acoustic image and the concept is the central one of language.[12]
Moreover, memory, which habitually and constantly calls up
connection between things and the sounds of words that signify
them, operates in a variety of ways. One of these is as storage. It
can register either the sound or the thing independently of
(therefore without) the occurrence of new sound waves being
carried to produce acoustic images.[13]

In poetry, language is shaped[14] to form a structure, and because words are sounds with meanings, what emerges can be
viewed as a whole, or sometimes (abstractly) as a sound structure, or, perhaps, as a meaning structure.

Cannot the same be said of rhetoric? In periods of history when
the art was sophisticated, not only was meaning programmed to
produce intensity of persuasion, but sound was patterned according to conventional rhythms for effects at sentence end-
ings.[15] Clearly, the radical difference between rhetoric and
poetry is found not in the means but in the end. Whereas the end,
or purpose, to which the process of rhetoric is directed is in the
addressee, that of poetry (making, shaping) is in the perfection of
the object made.

Thus a clearer analogy with poetry is seen in the shaping of a
form by a sculptor, or in a musician's composing of a sonata by
relating sounds. They "make" objects that did not exist before the

process. The goal of their efforts is perfection of the object taking shape, an extremity of desirability that, although not "useful" is profoundly valued.[16]

Knowing that literature *is not* rhetoric constitutes a big step forward. Knowing what it *is* is the logical next step. A method of discovery of the nature or "whatness" of anything whatever was proposed long ago by Aristotle. Discover what a thing is for (finality), who made it or how it originated (agency), what it is made of or constituted by (materiality), and how it is shaped or constituted (formality), and the theory of it, the knowledge of its nature, becomes clear.[17]

2
The Theory of Literature

Finality

THERE is not universal agreement that what I have said in chapter
1 is true. Terry Eagleton says "'pure' literary theory is an aca-
demic myth: some . . . theories . . . are nowhere more clearly
ideological than in their attempts to ignore history and politics
altogether."[1] This prompts an observation. As human beings we
all live in societies, nations, and alliances where the whole field
of politics is a reality, just as science, religion, and society itself
are realities of life. Literature will often *include* meanings that
are political, religious, philosophical, social. However, literary
theory is knowledge of what *literature* is.

Modern theories of literature, for instance, which claim the
expression of universal reality to be the purpose of poetry, date
back to Plato. He suggested the banishment of some poets from
the republic because their poetry, being imitation of a universal
transcendental world, referred to things twice removed from
reality.[2] They were removed from truth. Plato wanted those poets
retained in the republic who made hymns and panegyrics to
the gods rather than imitative constructs.[3] He thus assumed that
poetry, in order to be retained, should not be "removed" from
"reality." Prominent Neoplatonists, so-called because they too
focused attention on transcendent reality in connection with art,
have been numerous. Symbolists such as Blake, Shelley, Beaudelaire, and Rimbaud, and the American transcendentalists like
Emerson, considered the "end" to be in the neighborhood of
ultimate transcendental reality.[4] Yeats aimed to achieve an effect
akin to ultimate reality by the use of the symbol.[5]

"Expressionist" theories, on the other hand, locate the function in the *poet*, claiming poetry to be the expression of the poet's
feeling. Goethe, Burns, Wordsworth, Hazlitt, De Quincey,[6]
Amedée Ozenfant,[7] and others made this claim. A development
of the idea led to the delineating of the poet by looking closely at
the poetry, by "finding" Milton in his own works, for instance. It

could be, also, that critics (Yvor Winters, for instance) who have
traced the fault in a poem to be a failure in the poet as a person
instead of a fault in his art or his theory of what art should be,
could have been assuming expressionistic premises. The expressing of an amorphous, ineffable experience, said another
group of expressionists, could be achieved only by the use of
symbols. These included Mill, Hulme, Poe, Beaudelaire, Mal-
larmé, Rimbaud, La Forgue, Verlaine, and T. S. Eliot, among
others.[9] And a still later type of expressionism considered art to
be the creating of forms expressing the dynamics of feeling.
"Forms mirror the logic of feeling," as author Susanne Langer
said.[10]

That the "end" of poetry is in the listener or reader is another
very old idea, going back by implication to Plato.[11] It was confirmed, too, by a mistaken idea that this was the opinion of the
ancient poet Horace, who was popular in the seventeenth and
eighteenth centuries.[12] Many poets and critics throughout the
centuries have been convinced that poetry's function is to teach,
to delight, to uplift readers or listeners.[13]

The fourth alternative, that the end is in the poem itself, is
ancient and has been popular also in the twentieth century. The
poet makes the poem because he can and because "it shapes and
develops itself from within, and the fullness of its development
is . . . the perfection of its outward form.[14]

Poets, like painters of manneristic schools, cubists, and others,
have sometimes produced works for the sake of making perfect
specimens of a particular style. Imagists are among these. And
authors of the novel have sometimes bent their efforts toward
realism and exaggerated particularity in the use of the stream of
consciousness.[15]

The relatively small group who have considered poets and
other writers to effect the advancement of the future of the world
have been called Surrealists. They consider the poet to be a
seeker of the infinite,[16] looking forward to some prodigious
age.[17] There is, they claim, a natural connection between the
artist's subconscious and the world soul, or between the artist's
automatism and the automatism of the universe.[18] An artist's
automatic writing is thus a cosmic expression[19] that appeals to
hidden depths in the reader. The joining of his or her automatic
writing with the universe inaugurates a metamorphosis.[20] The
artist thus advances progress.[21] To facilitate automatic writing,
the poet induces a trancelike state, cultivates an irrational state of
mind, and thus is opened to an onslaught of images.[22]

That so many different concepts of the end, or function, of

poetry have been hot-headedly defended by so many gifted people suggests the subtlety and complexity of literature. Moreover,
arguments used by critics of opposing opinions are at least temporarily convincing. Probably the reason for this is that a poem is
"a locus of many values," to quote Sidney Zink.[23] Besides, artists, like the rest of us, may have their own reasons for doing
what they do. Keats wrote an excellent sonnet to a grasshopper to
win a bet with Leigh Hunt.

Regardless of readers or listeners, poets (still in the broad sense
to include novelist and dramatist), when beginning works, while
continuing them, and in finishing them, labor quietly and intensely to make something that requires their best. The works
themselves are the objects of their concentrated effort.[24] If sensing that their work could well have an effect on the reader pleases
them, we hope it does not sidetrack them. It is still the works
themselves that they want to make exquisite. If a poet manages in
what seems a miraculous moment to put a final touch that in-
vests a work with its own supreme actuality, his joy is indestruc-
tible.

Always, in such an instance, it is bound to have value for a
number of people and for a number of reasons; but "such an
instance" is not utilitarian. Its valuableness to several people is
not what the poet aimed at. What he wanted to do was to make
something perfect. If he or she achieved it, the primary value that
it has is "aesthetic."[25] Aesthetic value is desirable in itself, not
desirable as helpful to something else. It is an end in itself,
something we wish to stay to contemplate, not a means to some
other operative end. When the tragedy is so organized that all its
tragic complexity is held in a unity, the result will be, in the
audience, a catharsis of emotion. Similarly, when the sonnet is a
miniature universe where sounds and images variously hold
each other in their separate infinitesimal orbits, the result will be
unique and memorable. In fact, and to the extent that aesthetic
value qualifies the poetic structure, all the other numerous
values of the work will be potentially present in it. And aesthetic
values are the only values of which this can be said.[26]

The old saying that "a poet is born"—that the gifts that enable a
poet are "natural," and the process of making a poem is delicate—should be clear. However, both the poet and the poetic
process have been disputed.

Agency

Admirers of literature have written about the men and women
who have produced it, and many poets, dramatists, and novelists

have written about themselves and answered a variety of questions. A very brief sampling of differing opinions on a poet's distinguishing marks suggests their variety.

Plato claimed for the Greek epic and lyric poets "power divine" transmitted from the muse as through links of a chain, power by which poets were held and possessed.[27] The idea was continued by Neoplatonists and, although with a difference, by modern Surrealists. These latter claim that not a divinity but the "world soul" finds utterance in the release of the subconscious of the poet as "automatic writer."[28] Another modern and lateral descendant of the Neoplatonist line is the concept that all art is the result of the interaction of the moment, race, and milieu, and the poet is the mouthpiece of it. The pressure of the milieu (considered as damaging) on the poet is hinted at in an occasional modern commentary and by poets themselves. The "mad poet" has long been a stereotype.[29]

Another claim, made long ago by Strabo in conformity with an idea hinted at by Plato, was that a good poet has first to be a good person. The claim had echoes in the seventeenth, eighteenth, and nineteenth centuries. It has been at least implied in the twentieth century too.[30] Each of these long traditions, it seems, has its own appeal and each has had a considerable following. Their popularity can be explained by the fact that they can have some truth in them.

Meanwhile, an equally long and more central tradition, which seems more realistic, still survives in generally increasing strength. The ancient Greeks' words for *to make* (ποιεῖν), *maker* (ποιητής), a *making* or *forming* (ποίησισ), and *poetic* (ποιητικός) were used by Aristotle in his treatise on poetry to designate authorship of those particular kinds of poetry he had in mind (tragedy, epic, and comedy as well as products of other arts). The means a poet had to shape something with was "language alone,"[31] even though dance and music were sometimes enlisted in the theatrical performances and in recitation, as accompaniment.

It is characteristic, as Bate said, of "the classical attitude" to have less to say about the poet than about the product of his art.[32] It is certainly true of Aristotle who, in the *Poetics*, briefly indicated only two things (one twice implied concerning the management of plot, the other expressed once concerning metaphorical language)[33] distinguishing a poet from other men.

It is partly because *natural* gifts are hard to come by, because in fact there is no known way that a person without them can attain them, that we are prone to consider them "superior." Another reason is that natural gifts, as we know from the evidence, endow a person with the power to achieve seemingly miraculous results in areas of human endeavor. In the course of time a general word for natural propensity, *ingenium*, at first translated in a variety of ways, showed up in our modern word *genius*, applied to those who clearly excel.[34] In the realm of literature the term has a rich history, particularly, although not exclusively, in the romantic tradition. It has been considered synonymous with propensity to be inspired, intuitive, penetrating, effortless.

That genius in poets is characterized by those qualities when they are applying themselves to making poems everyone agrees. It is clear that "a poet is born." If poets are not people possessed (held, mouthpieces, or links in a chain from a divine muse to the audience),[35] if they are simply makers, the particular competencies that they have, enabling them to make poems, are indispensable.

Genius cannot be taught. It is natural endowment that enables a mathematician, an orator, a musical composer, a philosopher, a painter, or a poet to achieve excellence. But a mathematical genius is not a poetic genius, as most people would agree. Nature endows specifically. The particular genius of a person is identified by that person's particular exercise of art or science.

We use the word *scientist* for a professional knower and differentiate scientists from artists. However, the scientist exercises rational control (method) of the natural processes of learning, discovering, and proving. Science is "systematized conceptual knowledge."[36] The painter exercises control (by guiding rules and by intuition) of the natural processes of relating spatially (quantitatively) and with color and light (qualitatively). *Genius*, a word used to describe scientists, artists, and military leaders, is simply the extraordinary natural propensity enabling persons in different areas of endeavor.[37] Some people have genius in more than one area, as Leonardo da Vinci undisputedly had.

The poetic genius is naturally enabled to exercise rational control required to make a structure out of words, thus of sound and signification, by shaping a structure of sound that occasions a structure of meaning. The proof of genius is the work itself.[38]

Certain signs have been variously said to characterize persons of genius, independently of their works. These are intuition, greatness of spirit, an inclination to comprehend and esteem uncommon merit, a persisting incompatability with mediocrity, and a hankering after the utmost perfection of a work, whether slight or great.

"Inspiration"[39] aids a poetic genius in selection of materials. It is the stimulation of the imagination and fancy to invent. This stimulation is a response to both cognitive and affective meaning in life or in great literature. Poets themselves speak about it in a variety of ways, calling it "fire," "spirit," "rapture," "the muse," "bursts of freedom," or "effortlessness."

The most frequently expressed concept about the endowment peculiar to the poet, especially since the eighteenth century, is that of imagination. Some consider imagination to be the faculty of relating things with readiness. In the poet imagination is compelling and volatile, enabling a process of creatively dividing and recombining, or originating. It is a pervasive synthetic power. Literature about poetic imagination is vast and controversial.[40] Simply considered, it seems to be a faculty of registering mental images. It is a cognitive power, bearing only upon things that can be (not necessarily are) experienced by the senses, that are not purely intellectual. Imagination need not render things realistically: one can imagine huge things as miniature, for instance.

Imagination as such is not affirmation or denial, being distinct from intellectual judgment. The creative imagination, although it is one result of the activity of the intellect, is also influenced in its operation by emotion and possibly by the unconscious at times. A poet has a sensitive emotional apparatus. In lively associational play, and engaged within the frame of things that do not exist outside itself, imagination becomes fancy.[41] The crucial *expression* of a thought that "follows nature," namely *wit*,[42] is another faculty of synthesis.

Good poets have the analytical faculties of discriminating judgment aiding them to regulate the elements of their poems harmoniously; they have also taste, a judgmental sense guiding them in choices of the unprecedented for which no norm has been made explicit. Poets have an aptitude for words and a kind of expression considered as wit. The natural talents of poets include also what Pope called "the finest ear" and a predilection for the sound of words.[43]

In addition to natural endowment, some great poets have benefited by reading, by having acquired the assets of learning, by knowledge of the nature of literature, and by wisdom. However, poets of genius include some with and some without advanced education and reading. It seems from the survey of literature that without these advantages, the poetic impulse is more short lived, although there have been rare exceptions.

The poetic process, the gradual movement of agency begins in various ways: "How shall I manage this insight?" "What shall I make?" Or, the haunting of the mind by a word or phrase or a repetitive rhythm can begin some activity that eventually becomes the poetic process. The term *invention* was taken from rhetoric by critics of literature to designate what is referred to in a work.

However, the exercise of invention in poetry differs from its exercise in rhetoric. The use of the same word for the two different processes may well have been detrimental to theory. It was probably a carry-over from antiquity, when the effectualness of heroes' speeches in Homer's poetry was examined in the schools of oratory.[44] The word *invention* still appears occasionally in discussion about poetry, but in the poetic process it is less orderly than in the rhetorical. The poet does not, like students of rhetoric, find ideas first, then arrange them, and then word them. The awkwardness of the term for the poetic process has been regrettable.

A cluster of competencies constitutes a poet's natural endowment. When Shakespeare was called "myriad-minded" by T. S. Eliot, it was a reference to his copious inventiveness. Eliot attributed it to his propensity to "absorb knowledge," noting Shakespeare to have acquired "more essential history from Plutarch than most men could from the British Museum."[45]

Writers, too, have their own views of the world they inhabit and their own special interests. A novelist, it has been said, has a "good eye for a subject." Authors think "intensely and fruitfully" as they "haunt" the "world of creation." They "woo combinations and inspirations . . . by a depth and continuity of attention and meditation," wrote Henry James.[46] This is the general *habitus* or cast of mind of artists even when they are not creating a specific work. Sometimes a conception is tested and leaves a joyous satisfaction. Poets engage themselves with words in a relaxed, somehow receptive and primitive journey, making trial of words and meanings. Meaning at such a time is unpredictable in its occurrence, and ephemeral.

What starts the process, the germination, is often untraceable. An image or a phrase, a line of poetry, a rhythm, a vague echo, an idea of a plot, a concrete element of pictorial composition,— whatever the germ, it often comes unbidden like something given rather than deliberately chosen. It simply registers. Fielding, in his introduction to Book IX, chapter 1 of *Tom Jones*, calls it "a quick and sagacious penetration into the essence of . . . objects of contemplation." The circumstances of the moment when, unsolicited, the virus pricks, as James expressed it,[47] seem to differ with each work of art. One thing manifest in artists' accounts is that the subject might be borrowed from a particular reality or from no existent thing anywhere except as imagined in the mind.

The activity that immediately follows the germination in the mind is delicate. The poet, equipped by nature, senses the possibilities, is enamored of the "idea" (this word inclusively used for whatever it is, of all such things as those mentioned above whose coming is untraceable). A current of meaning gushes "full and clear"[48] to the poet's imagination. Novelists, dramatists, poets, composers, choreographers, painters—in short, artists, seem to agree on this phase of invention. James observed that there comes a "flash, upon the fancy, of a set of relations, . . . situations that, by a logic of their own, immediately fall . . . into movement, into a march or a rush, a patter of quick steps."[49]

The embryo is scant, he tells us, and at the same time there is a hint of obscure validity that compels confidence.[50] What is added to the work at this phase is often a "lucky find," and as the poet sees design in what is already coming together, new ideas occur. If these new ideas burden the slight, unfinished design they are swiftly consigned to a separate work for another day, or, if they compel attachment to them, the whole structure might shift its center. New determinations within the new elements invite others. Sometimes the process is slowed up. James tells us that after looking at "an aspect" of a character "under the lens for an hour" he saw it "give up its secrets," which "tumbled into the light."[51] The work thus advances considerably beyond the original germination, and in some instances, it proceeds rapidly.

Granville-Barker, speaking of Shakespeare's *Othello*, said "it seems" as though the characters were "pitching forward without the guidance or control of the author."[52] But there is making and thinking going on. Beiswanger, describing invention in the dance, says, "thinking deploys what making is to be and the making provides a manifest presence."[53] In the making of a play, this phase, as described to Bullough by a playwright, is moved ahead in a "struggle" between the "idea" and characters. The author works imaginatively and the "idea is sucked" up by the characters until "no trace of it is left outside the characters." In this complete fusion the idea undergoes change.[54] There are stretches also where the work is deliberately manipulated, of course.[55]

The magnetic principle that accounts for artists' sudden reach for an element to include is their intuitive and volatile sense of

its fitness or some aspect of connectibleness to what is already
there. The fact that the elements come uninvited to their minds
by a "logic of their own" does not mean that their minds are not
active, but rather that their activity is stimulated to a degree of
incandescence, and then flooded with joy in recognition of a rare
degree of fitness or aptness. The magnetism might appear to be
between a sound and a sound, an implicit question and a beckoning hint of an answer, or between any two elements whatever.

In that same cluster of competencies already referred to that
constitute a poet's natural endowment, is judgment. Judgment
controls and directs invention. The poetic process can err by
allowing invention to get out of hand. One can mar the perfect
work by including too much, or by including what lacks fitness.
Alexander Pope (who sometimes used the word *wit* to mean
invention) observed that "wit and judgment often are at strife"
although meant to be "each other's aid, like man and wife."[56]

The collaboration by which invention and judgment aid each
other in the poetic process can be illustrated by an analogy. Most
people have had occasion to observe someone expertly arranging
flowers in a vase. It is a process analogous to that of making a
lyric. The flowers are variegated in shape, in size, in color, and
for the present purpose they are compared to words or phrases.
Words differ in *shape* by being accented on the first, the last, or
an intermediate syllable. Some are short, some are long, some are
medium in *size*. The vowels and consonants constituting their
quality of sound are analogous to *color*, as many poets and critics
have observed.

The decorator chooses the type of bouquet, the general type of
flowers—large and brilliant, small and dainty, elaborate and
leafy. The choice is determined by several considerations—the
size and character of the niche (or table, or altar, or balcony, or
window sill) they will grace, as well as by the decorator's aptitude or taste. In the decorator's mind at this stage, invention and
judgment are in lively collaboration as possibilities rapidly occur
(invention) and are either banished or singled out (judgment).

The same is true in the selection of the vase or urn, in putting
the first principal flowers into it, as they fall into their own
postures depending upon their fiber and composition, and on
gravity. The effect of their mutual compliance and their stubborn
noncompliance mildly excites and challenges the decorator as he
or she adjusts them, adds others, inserts leafy sprays, combines
colors in analogous or complementary harmony. If a single spray,
or a group, stubbornly resists preference, the decorator might

empty the container and begin again or take out the recalcitrant elements or retain them and allow the sense of the whole to undergo pervasive change to a bouquet of a different character. The decorator's visual interest is imaginatively and radically engaged as he or she steps back to the "due distance" that "reconciles" the whole to "form and grace," as Pope said about viewing a painting.[57] This is a continuance of lively collaboration of invention and judgment.

The judgment has the final word in declaring the work complete, although sometimes without conviction at first as possibilities are still invited, appearing, and being rejected. As the charm of the uniqueness of the final result is experienced by the decorator, judgment applauds. The viewer is exhilarated, totally attached to the finished "effect."

Instead of flowers and leaves, the poet uses words of different shapes, sizes, and colors. In rhythmic combinations they seem to assume postures too, leaning, so to speak, in opposite directions (*beautiful*—ó o o, *on your guard*—o o ó, *humble*—ó o, *of course*—o ó).[58] These are quantitative in sound; and the vowel and consonant structures are also qualitative, analogous to soft or hard, or to color-saturated.

Poets make choices of the general character, the trend, of what they will create, depending upon factors difficult to locate that people their daydreams, and concerning which they spar to achieve for a variety of reasons. They might even have promised to produce a poem for a special occasion. They might be drawn to some image or lured by sounds of a phrase that continues to visit their minds.

Once they radically notice its promise and know clearly that they want to make a poem, they seize upon images, ideas, and words that they love—again for a variety of reasons. The elements might in themselves be commonplace or they might be rare and beautiful. Once they have the general idea of what to make, poets combine words, initially for their sounds perhaps, reject some words and find others, reaching for meanings in a state of excitement.

Invention and judgment collaborate, but because the elements, unlike flowers, are not fixed and visible but register in a poet's imagination as audible and meaningful, the process is a bit ghostly and its character disputed. However, as in the case of the flowers mentioned, where the combining and envisioning determined the selection and rejection of elements by invention and judgment, so too in the case with words: selecting, combining, and envisioning a whole, however nebulous, characterize the process. The finding, arranging, and wording are all melted into one in this activity, differing in this regard from the rhetorical process.

The feature of poetic invention that appears, in the perspective of time, to have become increasingly prominent, is the felt need on the part of the artist to achieve originality. Eighteenth-century critics repeatedly mentioned the fact that Shakespeare took the plots of his plays from old chronicles, from Plutarch, and yet he was astonishingly original. Had they stayed to penetrate this puzzling fact of their own observation, a clear analysis would have been widespread by this time, instead of an occasional insight of relatively few.

Samuel Johnson's Imlac, to prepare himself to be a poet, decided to acquire vast learning about many things and to travel to strange lands, because like some of Johnson's contemporaries, he thought that ancient literature had already included everything imaginable. Originality of invention was consequently difficult for poets who were his contemporaries.[59] When other factors combined with this, the difficulty of the search for originality was reinforced.

The success of the novelist Sterne became the occasion of a new tradition alongside the established one. The increasingly popular stream of consciousness seemed to offer opportunity for originality, and several talented novelists adopted it subsequently. The probing of the subconscious by poets, and by a long procession of artists, toward the unnatural and "surreal" has contributed to widespread suspicion that madness rather than "value" characterizes some of our modern literature and other arts. Among critics too, novelty appears to have become the criterion of excellence.[60]

Meanwhile, the astonishing originality and vitality of Shakespeare still appeals, as does that of a host of poets and novelists who have seemed unconcerned about originality and yet have managed to achieve it.

Originality does indeed crown the peak moment of a genuine work of art. And there is no secret about the accepted meaning of the word *originality*. The trouble spot is the nature of invention. To travel to strange lands and to pursue vast learning have their value, but not the particular value that an inventing poet (novelist, playwright, painter) needs. Rather, the novelist *imagines fully* the man in the book he is writing; he may be quite normal, no stranger from afar, no world leader, but a plain man, real or imagined. The important thing is thus not that he be different, but that *whatever* he is, the novelist knows him as though he were his living familiar. Because the man is precisely this kind of man, he is likely to want this or that or to avoid something else. Imagining him in the initial pursuit of his choice, the novelist turns his glance, so to speak, toward him *in* the pursuit. What occurs to the author's probing imagination might suggest further possibilities. One such possibility may be rejected for its doubtful plausibility; the other, a slim detail, may be retained. And once in the circuit this may appear more than a slim detail as a rush of new relationships with *it* gives it its own place in the narrative.

The principle of the rejection of the first and of the increasingly glad acceptance of the second is that of fit relationship: Relationship is what invention finds, not newness. Just before the moment of glad acceptance, moreover, it sometimes seems likely that there is a slimness in the new relationship. The novelist infinitesimally experiences anxiety, but as fitness begins to appear increasingly, it is transmuted to satisfaction.

Thus relation between the initial subject on the one hand and things superadded in the busy musing of imagination, things that *tumble* into the relationship, on the other, is the condition of the inventive process. Furthermore, it seems that there is a fragility, capriciousness, and doubt about a rapidly occurring image, hence a danger in seizing it. When nevertheless the artist has it firmly in the shaping work, if it begins to appear that for reasons he or she had not firmly thought of, the new thing is miraculously at home, related to freshly appearing aspects, and the "danger" overcome now works in reverse to warm the artistic process. The fitness of relationship is the crowning of the inventive effort.

Cicero, explaining the art of rhetoric, tells us that fitness, "which the Greeks called 'τὸ πρέπον,' is difficult to come by (*nihil est difficilior*).[61] The difficulty is not always from the scantness of beckoning possibilities. It can be caused by a number of conditions. Gifted and accomplished artists sometimes experience anxiety from the explosive principle in the subject, and constantly try to control the eager tendency toward expansion of a detail in the mind. The power of foreshortening is needed. In other words, judgment is indispensable.

Because fitness of relationship is the principle of invention, not differentness of things or persons included, originality should not appear too rare. Especially since it is fitness of only *aspects* of relationship rather than of things as wholes. Moreover, the principle holds in painting, sculpture, music, and dance, as well as in poetry. Relationship of aspects assures success to the inventive phase of any artistic process.

Ideally, judgment is unusually keen at peak moments of invention, coming to the rescue of fitness. It is sophisticated in the gifted poet, and early in the process it is guided by rules. By "early in the process" I mean in the earlier phases of making the poem.

Even to mention rules of poetic process is repugnant in large sectors of the present art world. The emancipation from classical rules had support from Young in 1759.[62] In antiquity, poets and critics considered "laws discovered" in the "nature of things" to have been agreed upon by men. Poets living as many as eight hundred years after Homer were encouraged to make Homer their study day and night,[63] so that they might grasp his methods of getting certain effects.

The romantic movement rejected rules, and its adherents rejoiced in their emancipation from classical and especially neoclassical rules.[64] Even T. S. Eliot, whose criticism and theory often had a refreshing independence, said that living poets should not be judged by the canons of dead critics.[65] This was a departure from classicism. The ancient respect for canons was not based on whether the critics enunciating them were alive or dead.

One of the reasons why rules were, and are, in such disrepute is that many people in the neoclassical period wanted to be critics but were ill equipped. It was fashionable to mouth the opinions of the most prominent, not always the most accurate, among them. The critics were satirized and the whole climate of the age became dissipated in time. Although Pope, the most aggressive and deadly satirist, was an intelligent supporter of the rules, he too was eventually drowned in the tidal wave of nineteenth-century romanticism.

Both of these historical trends played an important part in blurring the concept of originality. The fact is, however, that *originality is as available to the youngest of modern poets and artists as it was to the ancient Greeks and all those who came between.* Moreover, originality is likely to crown the work of the artist who uses rules in an early phase of creating a work.

In cooking, swimming, playing tennis, cleaning windows,

playing the piano, dancing, singing, and even blowing bubbles, there are ways of achieving the best effects. By being shown these or by discovering them by trial and error, one can gain competence. Noticing the difference between failure and achieving the best effects, and tracing the method by which one managed to get the desired effect, one is "discovering" a "law."[66]

This does not mean that anyone simply discovering it can apply it and thus create a work of art; Pope satirized such activity in "A Receit to Make an Epic Poem." Nor can one choose a rule blindly, nor is choosing the best rules a guarantee of excellence. The good poet uses rules as a means, never as an end. They are not rigid entities. They are principles abstracted by the judgment controlling the process wherever their use is appropriate. A rule of invention can promote excellence of invention, a rule of cadence, excellence of cadence.

Poets learn the rules of their art from one or both of two channels: from a good poem in which rules are implicit, or from theory already made explicit. Pope observed that Horace's "precepts teach but what his works inspire."[67] When poets learn from a poem they discover the nature of it. As the author of an ancient pseudo-Platonic dialogue said, "What . . . is . . . law? When things discovered are discovered, for instance, the cause of health and sickness by medicine . . . for art is surely the discovery of things, is it not?"[68] The rules that were implicit in works of Homer, Sophocles and Aristophanes were made explicit by Aristotle. They guided aspects of the nature of epic, tragedy, and comedy.

It is possible for a poet of rare good sense to derive rules directly from nature, the field of discovery. Nature is broader and deeper than the poetic process, which is contingent and particular. Moreover, rules never fulfill, they only "promote their end."[69]

Whereas nature's "lines" are "touched faintly,"[70] the rules expressing them, and thus making them clear, give security to the process of following nature. The control gained from intelligent use of the rules furthers the process, and what happens next, as a result, will almost inevitably be original. Pope used the phrase "grace beyond the reach of art," meaning the moment of seemingly miraculous achievement beyond any known rule. The unerring fitness of a shaping form to its own nature as this becomes specific expresses an intimate revelation of its nature that is savored and kept. It "becomes a rule."[71]

The rules of a process are thus norms of the nature of the process; rules of a poem are implicit norms of the nature of the poem as product of the process, not nature as a frozen absolute outside the poem. The rule made explicit can, it is true, assure another such process its right direction.

"Increasing fitness to its own nature" is an obscure phrase, but for the present purpose it means that a graceful poem at that moment of increase goes beyond itself and becomes the acme of grace. A tragic play at such a moment goes beyond itself and induces the extremity of the fearful catharsis; a sublime epic, the moment it outdistances the rules, actualizes a unique grandeur that can never find expression again; and a comedy at such a moment induces the extremity of laughter when the "sides split." These are moments of unique originality.[72] The poetic imagination, the swiftest of all things perhaps, achieves the mastery through *the* faultless word for that moment.

Invention in the poetic process can be clarified by observing what it is not. Samuel Johnson's idea of invention, namely the finding of persons and things to include in the literary work, differs from the above account in that the search is focused on things to be included instead of relatability to elements added earlier. Knowledge and experience constitute the principle of the first, whereas intuition of fitness is the principle of the second.

The opinion of Coleridge, although clearly on the side of fitness as principle, differs in another way from the above, however. Noticing the interior potential design of the shaping work, he likened the poem to a plant organism growing by its own life as determined in the seed, and the imagination of the poet as "growing" into its percepts, into internal relations of an "organic imagination."[74] It was indeed a good metaphor, but it laid too little stress on the *agency* of the poet, whose imagination, although volatile and lively, chooses deliberately as relatabilities occur to it, and works hands in hand with judgment, deleting as well as adding.

Freud's idea of the poet's work as imaginary satisfaction of unconscious wishes[75] focuses on *why* the poet's imagination selects, relating the elements to conditions of the unconscious. Although motivation by elements in the subconscious mind probably affects a healthy as well as a neurotic person, the inventive glance is directed to the poem being shaped, to the design emerging in the shaping of it. It claims intensity of the poet's *consciousness* busy on something newly appearing.

Freud's idea was anticipated in practice by the assent of many able authors, among them, Coleridge, Keats, Wordsworth, Shelley, Blake, Jung, and Schlegel.[76]

The mechanical theory of invention advanced by Hume and Hartley in particular considered remembered perceptions of the senses to be the source from which invention draws. Instead of reproducing these in the same spatial and temporal order as memory would, the poet's fancy and imagination were said to recombine them and unite them to form something new.[77] The idea of invention proposed in this study differs from theirs in that it extends invention to include the imaginary as well as the remembered reality; also, elements included show fitness of the relatability to the initial germ or the cluster of elements already taking shape as relationships accrue to it.

The principle of *association of ideas*, accorded wide acceptance by the successes of authors such as James Joyce and Marcel Proust, differs from the fitness in the above account of invention. Their concept was that the elements in the work of art are chosen from things somewhat arbitrarily *in the mind of the poet* rather than for their fitness to elements already joining in the poet's intuition of the poem's developing nature.

For the success of the genuine poetic process, a great deal is presupposed in the agent. The great poets, the great artists, are generally a people who understand their art and whose vision of life *appears* at least, judging from the excellence of their achievements, wide and unconfused.

Ancient orators who were trained in the technique of rhetoric learned invention—the finding of arguments, composition—the tactful arrangement of them, and then style or wording. But words[78] and their syntactic arrangement are, in the *poetic* process, substructures of the whole structure or form. Although structure as such is not meaning, every structure has a meaning peculiar to itself. The meaning of a poem that is a completed structure becomes clear once the structure is perceived. Something is expressed when the poem is realized as a whole. The poem can be rigorously analyzed by linguists, but the peculiarly poetic (aesthetic) structure as it is experienced *expresses* something that is necessarily natural.

Literature is made of language;[79] a statue is shaped of marble; a picture is formed of paint. And the language, the marble, and the paint, are designated as the material or "matter" of which these works are "made."[80] Language, marble, and paint are, in turn, already composed of materials that are further reducible to progressively simpler elements. At this present phase of advancement in linguistics, this is especially true of language.

Materiality

This inquiry, however, is directed away from these labyrinths to consider *taxis*, language primarily in its relation to structures that it makes up, specifically structures describable as poetic.[81] As linguistic processes these always include (1) a voice speaking, an address to someone or something, and (2) meaning conveyed by the words.[82] The *Iliad*, for instance, opens with an invocation by the poet to the muse; Tennyson's "Sweet and Low" is addressed by a mother to the "wind of the western sea." Such addressing is conveyed by words, that is, structured sounds (uttered or, as in reading, imagined) with specific meanings. These are shaped into the larger imagined structures of the plot of the *Iliad*, or the imagined yearning of the mother for the return of her sailor husband.

Meaning is relation.[83] More precisely, it is relation of reference. Initially, several axiomatic and practically self-evident statements can be made to clarify it.

1. Relation as such never pertains to one thing only. There must be a thing that relates and a thing it is related to. Rarely do we find meaning, especially in literature, in this simple condition; there is usually multiplicity of relationship. Nevertheless, *as such*, relation requires at least two poles of reference. The leaf is related to the branch. The sound of the word *cat* is related to the animal that is signified.
2. Things that are related are things that have something in common or some basis on which they can be seen as related. The leaf and the branch are parts of the same tree. The sound of the word *cat* and the meaning reference to that animal are elements of the same signification. One is a sign or designation of the other.
3. Things related are never identical. Relationship presupposes that the related things are distinct. The leaf is not the branch. The word *cat* is not the animal. Even should related things look identical, like two grains of sand, they are "one" and the "other," individuated. Under the microscope they do not even *look* identical. Or, your own image in the most perfect of mirrors is distinct from you. One is a reflection that is a condition of light, and the other is you.

4. The idea "another" implies the correlative "one" *simultaneously*.
5. Relationship is not necessarily between the composition of one thing and the composition of another. It can be between one *aspect* of a thing and an *aspect* of the other. In the sentence, "The wet street unfurled like a ribbon," the relationship is between the shining of the street (not the asphalt itself) and the shining of the ribbon (not its weave).
6. Relationship is actual only when it is apprehended by someone. In reality (independent of anyone's ability to apprehend) there is only relatability, not relationship. When it is said that meaning is relationship of reference, the word *reference* presupposes the apprehension.

Poetry is made of words. A word is a little complex of sounds with a certain conventional signification or "meaning." The material that poets work with has in itself already been organized in four different ways: by arrangement of consonant and vowel sounds; by arrangement into sounds of syllables and sounded words; by conventional attachment of significations to these to form words; and by arrangement of these words into syntactical constructs.

The arrangement of consonant and vowel sounds is done by differentiating, just as the sculptor's making the marble into the form of a bird is done by chiseling away or separating whatever in the block of marble is not of a bird's form from that which is. In the organizing of a word's sound there are only differences, qualitative and quantitative. The same is true in the forming of an expressed idea. The mind focuses on it, discriminating or separating from it all that is not it.

However, the sign or word that comprises both the sound signifying and that which is signified, is a positive term (as de Saussure explained, sound *signifying* plus the idea or thing *signified* equals the *sign*, or word[84]). So a word, in itself a form in which elements are related, signifies or refers to something. It "means" it.[85]

It may have occurred to the attentive reader that sound is a physical thing and an idea is not so. The fact is that *both* the sound and the thing signified are registered in the reader's or listener's *mind*. True, when a word is spoken, physical sound waves are set in motion and travel to the listener's eardrum. But from the vibrating eardrum the auditory nerve carries the impression of the sound to the brain, where it is registered as an auditory image. As I said earlier, between the auditory image and the idea signified by it is the precise locus of the brain where language is constituted. It is where the *image* of the sound *(signifiant)* and the *image* of the thing conventionally associated with it *(signifié)* are instantly related: meaning is actualized.

Language is necessarily conventional. It is because listeners are in agreement about what the signs (words) signify that the message is intelligible. Language exists to convey meaning. Even when conventionality is attributed to ordinary spoken language, that is not disputed.

However, the language of poetry has long been a matter of dispute. In order to understand the question it is necessary to approach it step by step. I have already taken a few indispensable steps, and perhaps they might bear brief summarizing: (1) poetry is speech *(parole)*; (2) speech is made of words, that is, sounds signifying and things signified; (3) the signification or meaning is largely conventional; and (4) the meaning is *actualized* in the *mind* in the association of the auditory image with the image of the thing signified. The association is conventional.

Conventionality is established by one means or other. People who dress conventionally follow established patterns of dress. People of conventional manners conform to an established order of behavior. By *established* is meant agreed upon by many people, explicitly by published fashions and by laws, or implicitly by fairly universal and lasting custom. How the conventional significations of words came to be established constitutes another totally different, large question, investigated by some students of linguistics and of ancient and medieval etymologies. That linguistic signification is conventional is indisputable.

However, meaning can be conveyed naturally as well as conventionally. When people are not following an established pattern, something else dictates their dress or behavior, and it is often likely to be the nature of the situation—the weather, or their own particular personal natures. *Nature* is a broader term than *convention*. Some conventions are founded upon nature, that is, gradually followed because to perform them is natural, agreeable to the nature of the person doing them, or conducive to an agreeable natural outcome. Other conventions are not based on nature but are followed as "fads."

Language is not the only conveyor of meaning. The appearance of the sun above the horizon *means* that day is at hand. A visual image of pallor in the sky is conveyed by the optic nerve to the brain. It is associated by experience with the idea of day's arrival.

Again, it is the mind that is the locus where the meaning is actualized. If no mind receives it, the two things are more accurately designated as *relatable*.

The locus, then, of both natural and conventional meaning is the mind. Nature or convention or both supply the mind with relatable images.

Because the nature of language is basic to the nature of normal discourse and rhetoric and of poetry, there have been instances of dispute about the language of poetry. The poet Wordsworth claimed that it is the language of the common man, a claim contradicted by Coleridge. Poetic language, said Coleridge, is somehow extraordinary.[86]

Wordsworth was interested for a good while in the French Revolution, favoring the common man in his politics. But it has been recognized that Wordsworth's poetic achievement was more notable when the language of his poetry departed from the manner of the common man's language, also, that what Wordsworth produced as intentionally "common" was not in fact so.[87]

Poets use a great variety of figures of speech, archaisms, inversions ("out of the sea came he"), alliteration, assonance, rhyme, and so forth. Thus, while words remain words, the poet often uses them in an uncommon way. Whereas normal speech is conventional, poetic speech is often, although not always, found to be natural and even unconventional.

Moreover, whereas the signification of a word is denotative, it can also be connotative when other things associated with it come to mind. For instance, *water* can "connote" the quenching of thirst, floods, freshness, coolness, oceans, dripping faucets, and so on. The denotation is conventional. Connotations, although they can be conventional, are more properly natural.

Whereas the language of pure prose, such as that of a scientific treatise, has a maximum of denotation and a minimum of connotation, poetic language *as such* has a maximum of connotation and a minimum of denotation. The reason for italicizing *as such* is that even the best of poets do not always use poetic language. Particular moments invite particular choices. Nevertheleless, it is useful to notice that poetic language is connotative and suggestive, and in that particular feature it can be said to be natural rather than conventional.

The poetic figure onomatopoeia departs from the usual use of language. The thing conventionally denoted by the words is also suggested by their sound. For example:

The fair breeze blew,
The white foam flew,
The furrow followed free.
We were the first
That ever burst
Into that silent sea.

The stanza from Coleridge's *Rime of the Ancient Mariner* denotes the ship moving swiftly on a deserted open sea, breaking the surface, the prow throwing the foam back. The sound of foam is like *f*, and when the foam breaks it suggests the sound *s*. The foam created by the ship's prow cutting the water is suggested in the f-f-f-f-f-f-s-s-s-s (*fair-foam-flew-furrow-followed-free-first-burst-silent-sea*). The clarity of sound uncluttered by other sounds further emphasizes the scene.

The rudimentary things that have been said about meaning can be summarized here. The "voice" or imagined speaker in a literary work can be inferred from the meaning of the words themselves. Meaning is the relationship of one thing referring to another, actualized when apprehended by the mind. Words exist to refer. Language, largely conventional, is generally intelligible. Literature is speech, spoken or represented as spoken. The meaning is sometimes conventional therefore, but the language that conveys its meaning is not ordinary. Poets use figures and devices in ways not found in ordinary language. Poetic language is less denotative and more connotative, and in that sense more natural than the language of prose. Onomatopoeia illustrates the ability of language to denote a meaning conventionally and at the same time to mimic the denoted thing by its sound. In such mimicry usage is not conventional but natural.

Having considered the finality, agency, and materiality of literature, we approach the most central of the four questions, which relates intimately to the first. What is form? What is literary form? Why is knowledge about it central to understanding literature?

Formality

Understanding form is indispensable to understanding literary theory. A form of anything at all is the totality of relations among elements. In recent decades the words *structure* and *elements* have seemed preferred to *form* and *matter*, having been adopted by physical scientists. The more recent usage is clear and convenient enough for our purposes.

In art (defined a while back as "rational control of natural process"), structure is imposed on elements supplied, ultimately at least, by nature. That the elements are not always supplied directly by nature, as the sculptor's marble is, is obvious. The paint used by the artist, the steel and concrete of the builder following the plan of the architect, are already processed. And as for the material from which literary structures are made, although the sounds and the organs that produce them are physical and natural, language is conventional and formal. Its own elements are various and numerous sounds, and various and numerous things signified. A poem is shaped of these. It includes the "forms of language and is . . . conditioned by and dependent upon them," as La Drière observed.[88] Thus, the form or structure of a poem is in fact a structure of substructures.

The imposing of form on materials is done in two unlike ways, namely, by differentiating and by adding. For instance, the whistling of a tune achieves form by differentiating E from D, D from C, D from E. Or the carving of a man out of marble is a taking away of the excess marble that is not part of the form of a man. Such differentiating, taking away, separating, is the first way in which form is imposed on the sound of words.[89] The sound of *alone* is perceptible as a structure because the phoneme /ə/ differs from the phoneme /l/, which differs from /o/, and /o/ differs from /n/. And the degree of loudness of the stressed syllable *lone* differs from the unstressed syllable *a*. It is already a structure. However, the concept signified (alone) is different in its signification from other concepts, from the concept *accompanied,* for instance. Thus, both the sound signifying and the significations of words are in themselves little structures.

On the other hand, a word as a formed sound with a precise signification is a more complex structure. It illustrates the *other* way in which structures are imposed on elements, namely by adding. The sound that signifies plus the meaning that is signified constitutes the sign, that is, the word. Craig La Drière said parenthetically to an English Institute audience at Columbia University on one occasion, "All structure is ultimately reducible to sameness and difference."

In the sound of a whole line of a poem, structure is observable in the arranging of different elements of sound and silence, and in the accenting and nonaccenting of syllables. Sameness is seen too in repetition of qualitative sounds as in alliteration, assonance, consonance, and rhyme. Moreover, the syntactical arrangement of words occasions intricate and sometimes far-reaching structure. Meaning structures are occasioned not only by the significations of the words but also by the sound structures themselves. It is in when actually considering an eminently successful poem that all of these somewhat abstracted reflections are confirmed and rewarded.

As I said above, a form is the totality of all the relations among the elements. In nature there are millions of relatabilities, not relations. They are, of course, different and distinct from non-relatabilities.[90] It is possible for relatabilities, unlike non-relatabilities, to *become* relations, but the mind is indespensable to the actualizing of relationship. The mind perceives the relatabilities in realities and thus relates them.

Not only does the mind actualize relationship in discovering relatability in nature, in the world, in people, in situations everywhere; it can invent it where it does not exist; it can imagine it.

Moreover, whenever two things are found relatable, what is relatable is only an *aspect*, or aspects, of each, not the things in their totality. A reflection on a sunny wall will repeat the shape of the forsythia spray nearby. The wall has its own character: concreteness, grayness, roughness, weight, consistency, relative permanence, immovability, and rectangularness. The forsythia has its own short history from seed time to that moment: its own growth, moisture, color, multiple figuration, and suppleness. But the *aspect* figuration or shape of bent spray on the wall and the *aspect* of bent spray of the bush are relatable. The mind perceives the visual impression of the sight of the structural resemblance which has a whatness of its own then, increasingly inviting attention. Once the mind has discovered it, there is actual relation.

When the mind has actualized relation between aspects of things in reality, it has not changed that reality. (It does, of course, change the state of the discovering mind.) The essence of relationship is simply the being *referred* to another not itself.

In a form such as that of a novel or a play, a structure actualized in temporal sequence (plot), the occurrence of an event referred to can be perceived as being over before the beginning of the resulting occurrence. But the mind (memory) retains the impression of the first occurrence while it is reading or watching the resulting one. The impressions can thus be apprehended as parts of a form, because in response to the novel or play, the correlations are simultaneous. Meanwhile, in a plot, the incident that resolves suspense is not the only thing that conditions the response: all that might have happened, all too that kept the reader waiting, is included in the impact of the resolution. In fact, in literature generally, relatabilities such as connotations and suspense possibilities not actualized hover about the actualized relations, more properly in the reader's shadowy response. The related elements, moreover, do not suggest themselves to the mind arbitrarily. They must be for some reason assimilable.

Even while elements, by being relatable and assimilable, are predisposed to formality, they also show oppositions or contrasts that conduce to intensity and to reciprocity. Response includes seeing parts as means to the whole (which is contemplated with conscious retentiveness of parts), and then seeing the whole as a means to a part, that is, noticing a part's particularity and extendedness, at the same time holding on to the totality.

Elements in other words, have a predisposition, for one reason or another, to formation, The form is achieved by the organization of the elements into a unity. Each element is its own special self, has its own particular effect, contributing at the same time to the singleness of the whole. The whole is "single" in the final effect, although multiple in the number of variety of its aspects. The single final effect is unity.[91]

Where there is unity there is dominance and subordination. A dominant aspect is enjoyed if there are numerous and compelling subordinate aspects. Dominance and subordination characterize not only individual elements but norms of a whole structure as well. The principal norm aids the subordinate. For instance, in the line uttered by the banished Duke Senior, "Sweet are the uses of adversity,"[92] the principal norm is his expressing realization of his good fortune where ill fortune might have been expected. That is, the meaning. But there are other less noticeable norms. A person could have expressed the same kind of realization by saying, "After all that, we're lucky." In Shakespeare's line there are aspects that tug at attention although we do not direct notice toward them. They are norms of style, grammar, and prosody. It is perfectly good grammar to say, "The uses of adversity are sweet," but in the pleasant deviation from normal word order by the inversion, an effect of impulse of the Duke's realization is achieved. The "sweetness" of his present position is freshly dawning on him. The grammatical normality has given in to the special style norm with the result that the meaning is given prominence. The word *uses* too illustrates the truth that each element is its own special self and has its own particular effect. *Uses* is a plain word between *sweet* and *adversity*, which are not, and yet it applauds adversity. The effect is an increase in meaning: its homeliness has a familiarity that supports the impression of friendship of the Duke for his followers to the Forest of Arden, and adds to his charm. And there is mild pleasure felt in the centrality of the paradox, of negative adversity and positive sweetness. This adds to the meaning.

So too does the prosodic structure, which gives accent to the word *sweet* and gives the dominant accent in the line to the syllable *ver* of *adversity*, supporting the meaning that the unexpected sweetness of life in the forest seems incredible to men who have endured so much suffering. *Uses*, having two syllables, is a spilling over of feeling of the Duke's monosyllables, and the dike threatens to give way, so to speak, in the four-syllable *adversity*.

The line is a small substructure of the whole structure of the play. It has a universality of meaning for humans, who often experience the paradox. But it adds to the line itself and to the whole structure of the play to note that the unified meaning of the whole plot is mirrored in the meaning of the line uttered by the Duke.

A form, as was said, is a unified structure of substructures. In artistic structures, subordinate norms declare themselves, and yet hierarchy is maintained. The relation of one substructure to the others is *usually* of greater import than the relation of one element to the other, important though that can be.

Craig La Drière distinguished two kinds of order or organization, namely, series and system. A series is an order of recurrence tending to diffuse an identity that has been established, whereas a system is a cumulation.[93] Another distinction is that between macrostructure and microstructure.

Macrostructural and microstructural elements of a work must be assimilable, and aspects of things referred to by the words are relatable, thus contributing to the unity of the meaning structure. Although relationship on which unity depends is not actual except by the mind's apprehending relatabilities, the unity of the structure is real. René Wellek, when he said a poem is "a system of potencies,"[94] was referring to something real (potencies are real), and by his use of the word *system* he meant unity. The actual unifying of it occurs in the mind. The person seeing (thus actualizing) relationship of fitness of one element to another, then another, and another, gradually experiences a sense of unity. Accordingly, as this grows out of the relation among aspects (elements), the norms of fitness (the way it is shaping) become

increasingly defined and clear. This not-as-yet-complete structure begins to be recognized as having a character, a nature, or
whatness of its own.

The norms are objective, that is, originating as the *way* the
object is taking shape. Their source is the fitness of one aspect of
something already included (a sound or a meaning) to another,
and this to another, and these to others. In other words, the
norms are objective because they originate in the fitnesses of
elements in the object. They are intrinsic because they originate
in the nature or whatness of the object and terminate in the
completion of its nature. The progress toward actualization seeks
itself. The thing makes its own demands.

This, I suspect, is what T. S. Eliot meant when he wrote,
concerning the poet in the process of making a poem, that "what
happens is a continual surrender of himself, as he is at the
moment, to something which is more valuable."[95] Obviously, the
poet, being human, is more valuable, but the emerging nature of a
shaping poem imposes norms that cancel out the expressing of
himself, if such expressing is irrelevant to what the form is
progressing toward being. The word *norms* need not present a
difficulty. It is a better word here than *rules*, because rules are
usually explicit. The meaning of the word *norms* is given a
certain clarity in Schrecker's remark that what appears as structure in the product operated as norms in the process that made or
caused it.[96] Norms are ways of bringing something about. As the
structure takes shape, there is a clarification of the norms according to which actualization *should* take shape.

To repeat, the nature of a thing includes not only its actuality
but also its potencies or propensities. Also, between an actuality
(or *act*, as philosophers used to say) and its potency, the relationship is characterized by necessity.[97] Thus, a person has a
sense of what it can become. Expectancy attends the apprehension of the occurrence of a word, a phrase, or an eventuality.

Perhaps the concept of poetic structure will need further clarification. What remains to be seen will appear in the consideration of value, and especially that of aesthetic value as such, of
values proper to particular types of aesthetic structure in literature, and finally will appear in the exemplification of aesthetically valuable structures in specific literary works.

Value is not a simple property. As Laird said, "Relations are the
breath of value."[98] The reader who follows the next few pages
will, I suspect, agree. However, at the end of the account the

concept of value will be clear enough to be defined with relative simplicity and then exemplified.[99]

Elsewhere I have attempted to answer the questions: What is value? What is aesthetic value? How is it distinguished from other values?[100] I want to restate some conclusions here before treating two further questions (What are the aesthetic values? How is each defined and exemplified in literature?) that pertain more precisely to this particular study. The magnitude and disputedness of these questions prohibits lengthy explanation of other opinions cited, and the serious reader will do well to resort to the bibliography.

3
Value

WHAT is value as such?

1. Among other things, it is a condition present in something, *enabling it to satisfy a requirement or desire*. In a sudden downpour it is an umbrella; for comprehending the meaning of an obscure word it is a dictionary; for shopping it is money; for relieving thirst it is cold water.[1] *The wished-for thing has "value" that borrows its character partly from the nature of the wish.* If the umbrella does not open, if the dictionary page is torn and the meaning of the particular word is lacking, if the money is foreign or in a lost wallet, or if the water is polluted value is not actualized. The reach for the umbrella, the dictionary, the money, or the water originates in recognizing the ability of each of them to satisfy a desire or a felt lack.
2. Value resides in a particular aspect of the desired object—in protectiveness from rain, in the availability on the page of the dictionary definition, in the exchangeability of the money, and in the purity and coldness of the water.
3. The value's occurrence is real, being available and actual. The valued thing has some capability, some "virtue" that is due to a perfection of its nature or a power in its action. It is exemplified in the size and shape of the umbrella, the intelligibility of the definition, the undisputed exchangeability of the money, and the coldness and purity of the water. The resulting virtue of each of these to satisfy is, respectively, serviceability, clarity, purchasing power, refreshingness.
4. *The particular perfection ascribed to the nature of a thing, enabling it to satisfy, is the result of the principle of its organization, and its power is felt in its effect:* protection by the umbrella, clarity and relevance of the dictionary definition, easy exchange provided by the money for a service or a commodity, and refreshment provided by the water.
5. The reach for the valued object is directed partly by a per-

son's knowledge or intuition of the virtue or ability of the object to satisfy. There is a concrete promise in the object, a potency, and an intuitive hope bearing upon a particular. The lack prompting a reach for the valued object is a desire for actualization. If it is not actualized, the value is nonexistent.

Because the nature of a thing is the principle of both its actuality and its potentialities, and because the correspondence between an actualized thing and its propensities (potencies) is governed by necessity,[2] we expect particular potentialities from something actual, sometimes on the basis of experience and sometimes by intuition.

6. A reach for something that will satisfy is directed to the means, the satisfaction being the end or purpose. The question of means and end, although it is not the whole story, is helpful to understanding of value. The word *end* used correlatively with the word *means* designates a representation of something (a desirable possibility) to the mind. It comes first to mind as a motivation, although it is fulfilled last. End is therefore intentionality. It is both an image of the hoped-for thing and a director of the process of making or obtaining (realizing) the object.

Sometimes a promise is only one phase of a series of means-end processes. For instance, a law student studies in order to pass the examination,[3] passes the examination in order to get credit, and gets credit in order to get a degree. The student gets a degree in order to apply for the bar examination, and this in order to be licensed, and this in order to practice law.

7. Pertinent though the idea of means-end correlation is to the idea of value, the value of a thing includes more. Each means-end unit is single, each is required to be in its right place, and the series is a completed whole. *It is the value of the last end in a series that confers unity on the series.*

What makes an end available is the "virtue" of the means:[4] the intelligence and thoroughness of the young person's study, the relevance and authority of the examination, the authenticity of the credit earned, the authorization gained by the degree, the scope and relevance of the bar examination, and the validity of the license to practice. The unity conferred on the series, like unity of anything, presupposes principality and subordination, and the exceedingness of its value gives the last end in a series principality. Such "exceedingness" is due to the specificity of the need or desire behind the reach.

8. Order is implied in unity, and it is present in a series of means-end processes when each is in its place. Order is always required for the presence of value. Its unifying principle is the influence of the "final cause," or end, conceived as purpose—the young man's initial image of himself practicing law. In the series he does not practice law in order to apply for the bar examination.

9. Order, said Aquinas, is "due adaptation of means and end."[5] Its sanctions are immanent, that is, only *if* this particular proportional means is applied will this proportioned end be the result. The end or purpose overcomes contingency or arbitrariness and is the foundation of reasonableness.

10. Value is a condition of structure, so relation is important to it. Moreover, several values can be ascribed to an object at the same time. In such a case there is order in the network of relations.

11. An object that is valuable always belongs to a system: The umbrella mentioned in (1) through (4) above belongs to a circumstantial system, the dictionary definition, to a linguistic system, money, to a government's monetary system, and the water, to the physical systems of its composition and temperature.

12. Since a valuable object belongs to a system, it stands related to it. But it stands related at the same time to another system (or systems) behind a valuer's lack.[6] For instance, a glass of milk (behind which there are chemical systems) satisfies hunger behind which there is a physical system of subordinate systems (digestive, reproductive, circulatory, nervous, respiratory). The workable umbrella satisfies the need for dryness required for the combination of circumstances demanding it. The clarity of the dictionary definition makes it apt for the system of the intelligible sentence, and the pure cold of the water makes it apt for its energizing and refreshing physical operations.

13. What this comes to is simply that a valuable object or occurrence is always related to at least two systems or groups of systems.

14. Value emanates from the uniqueness or purity of a particular aspect of the valuable object. Uniqueness in a valuable occurrence is borrowed partly from the valuer's lack or desire and partly from the exactness and purity (freedom from alloy or disorder) of the moment when satisfaction is actualized. The purity results when the system, of which the valuable is

an expression, is most fully behind it, that is, best represented by it. This system is usually more stable than that or those behind the valuer's lack, as it is frequently (not always) established independently of, and before, the valuable occurrence. For instance, the money system behind the coin has its existence in human minds, being the order of interrelationship. The system is organized, often written down or recorded in some way, perhaps expressed in routine action, as there is a relative fixity about it.

15. The systems that are related to a value occurrence undergo increase and adjustment, and the valuable object enjoys a new and particular relationship.

16. Value, said La Drière, is "relation apprehended as requiredness."[7] The reach of the valuer's mind (apprehended) is one of the elements related. This is meant by the word "due" in Aquinas's definition. Value can be conceived of as a locus where system meets system.

Sometimes clusters of systems are interrelated and linked with the valuer's desire or felt lack. This can be exemplified by the cluster of systems involved in the value of a diamond. A diamond is an object related to systems it expresses, a final outcome of a collaboration. Involved are: carbon, the energy of the sun and all the factors, hydrogen presumably, in the proper circumstantial conditions, which result in the energy of the sun; aeons of development; complex physical and chemical distillation to a required precision of mixture; the result in complex atomic composition with all its causes; and a molecular change under various influences to a precise equilibrium. It is thus an expression of converging systems.

Diamonds are relatable to other systems too. Owing to their hardness they are useful for cutting glass and are sought out by glaziers who, in turn, are suppliers of commodities. Rare and relatively difficult to get, diamonds have great exchange value for merchants, who operate according to regulatory systems. And, cut with exactness by masters, they have brilliance and complexity and are valued for their beauty.[8]

Each of these systems of relatability is actualized when those who seek the diamonds recognize their usefulness to them. Even a diamond's beauty can be utilitarian if sought by someone mainly for social occasions. When value is present to an object or situation, it is a meeting of some systems behind the valued thing and other systems behind the valuer.

However, value occurrence is not *burdened* with systems. The experience of value is enjoyable. Systems need not be adverted to, and relationships are largely intuited. The valuer gradually comes to realize them at least partially and often retrospectively. They open up in the dynamic contemplative process of valuing.

4

Aesthetic Value and Affective Hazard

WHAT I have said in chapter 3 pertains to both utilitarian and nonutilitarian values. It is time to consider the latter, aesthetic value, which is primary in literature.

Aesthetic value is a condition that makes the object desirable, but the desire is simply to continue looking at the object, to contemplate it. This is true of any object of fine art, as of many objects in nature. That aesthetic value can characterize both art and nature is due to the fact that the fundamental difference between a beautiful natural object and a beautiful art object is the source. We pause to look at a rose or a rainbow in nature, and to contemplate a beautiful painting made by art. Our wish to continue looking at the painting is not utilitarian: we do not want to wear it or eat it. Even should we want to sell it, or "use" it to decorate a room, this is feasible because it already has aesthetic value.

Such value inheres in the structure of the rose, the rainbow, or the painting.[1] All the relatabilities, all the systems, are part of the structure. The fitness of part to part and the fitness of parts to the whole unify it. This is easy to apprehend when one thinks of a rose, a rainbow, or a painting. Some, it is true, might answer that when they see a rainbow or a rose they think of a transcendent reality—God or nature. But in such a case, the cause is probably the presence of aesthetic value, and this alone is what is being defined. The adverting to transcendence is another step to another realm, namely the ultimate cause, which is not, as such, a substitute for aesthetic character.

In literature, because language has meaning, it may seem to some readers that the literary object is one thing and that the meaning soars up and away like a balloon. But the fact is that the organized meaning, the organized sound, and the organized interrelatedness of these together constitute the object made of language.[2] Its perfection is the result of the principle of its organizational structure, and its power is felt in its effect on the perceptive reader.

His reach, perhaps directed initially by knowledge of the reputation of the author of the poem, soon becomes an intuitive expression of a particular possibility. And once in the current of meaning he reaches for some actualization. Value attends the actualization, assuming the conditions of value to be present.[3]

If the meaning is dynamic, that is, constituted to form the plot of a story, a novel, or a play, the reach is for an immediate means in a means-end process. For instance, curiosity is aroused concerning the "thing" that the guards of Elsinor Castle are thinking of telling Hamlet. The reader reads on. It becomes clear from their words that the ghost of the late king walks about the castle at night. This is an *end* of the means that was the whispering of the guards. When suddenly the ghost appears, their reaction of fear is a *means* of signifying that it portends some horror, and they ask Horatio to speak to it, but it stalks away. This, plus the fact that it resembles Hamlet's father, the dead king of Denmark, increases their curiosity and ours. Horatio says he will inform Hamlet of the apparition since it is more likely to speak to the young prince. These developments constitute a series of means-end processes organized to actualize a *suspense value*.

The connected series of these imaginary events embodied in the meaning is important to the whole construct. Each constitutes a means to an end, namely the *next* event, which once expressed becomes a means to the next, and so forth.[4] The adherence of the mind in curiosity is a kind of desire, a reach for satisfaction; but it is not aesthetic. The total structure of the meaning is so organized as to express "the tragic," which is an aesthetic value that can characterize a meaning structure. But the tragic includes many more elements than simply the sequentiality that effects alternating suspense and satisfaction. The apt unifying of a whole network of expressed and implied systems is characterized by order, indispensable to the aesthetic value of a tragedy as to all aesthetic values, and to value as such.

Aesthetic value differs from other kinds of value in two respects: it inheres in the form, either natural or created by art; and the reach, suspense, or felt lack of the valuer is induced by the organization of the elements of the valued object itself.[5] The aesthetic object, therefore, is valued not for the sake of an end outside it. The aesthetic structure itself is the end. It is desirable in itself and invites continuance of contemplative process.

Some of the systems united in an occurrence of utilitarian or functional values are fairly fixed and stable, and we therefore understand them before we understand a particular value occurrence. In aesthetic value, on the other hand, the systems are uniquely orginated. They co-occur.

Since aesthetic values are valued in themselves, not for ends outside themselves, they must be caused by the relationship of the parts to each other. Moreover, being "desirable," they have an effect on us.

There is indeed a special condition about relationship in objects of art as well as in nature and in "life" that excites the human mind that apprehends it. In a work of art, the condition is present among the elements within the boundaries of the work itself. It is caused by relationship, the only phenomenon at all besides the elements. And since relationship is present among all sorts of things that do not particularly excite observers, something that characterizes the relationships constituting art objects must be caused by a condition of their organization. Thus the question is narrowed: What is the condition?

Relationship among elements of anything at all presupposes the presence of five elements: (1) something that relates, (2) something it relates to, (3) whatever is common to these as a basis of relationship, (4) factors not common to them, tending to keep them distinct or separate, and (5) a mind that apprehends the relationship between them and, implicitly, their separateness or difference. Related *things* (the word enlisted for want of an adequately inclusive term) might be aspects of things, moments of time, ideas, sounds, shades of color, or practically anything. Sometimes the discovery of relatability is exciting and affective; sometimes it is not. Clearly, the question is, what condition is present in affective or exciting relationship and absent from relationship that is not?

The answer is to be found in the fourth of the abovementioned factors, namely "reasons why the relatable things are not identical, everything that keeps them separate."[6] Whatever tends to keep the relatable things separate must be very great to constitute an obstacle or hazard to relationship.

Because recognition of relationship *despite* hazards to it is exhilarating, it is convenient to call a felt obstacle to relationship *affective hazard,* as I have done elsewhere.[7] The principle of affective hazard is this: The greater the sum of all that is *not* common to terms that have something in common, and hence the greater the obstacle to their union, the more affective or exciting is the apprehension of their union; or, the more unrelatedness there is, the more exciting the discovered relatedness is. The afective feeling does not replace cognition; it is feeling that attends it. Aristotle noted in his *Poetics* that it is "natural" for all men to "delight" in imitation.[8] The delight arises, I am suggesting, from seeing relation between terms that are not identical by nature. A natural obstacle that separates them can never be annihilated. Related things might be aspects of things, moments of time, ideas, sounds, shades of color, meanings, numbers, practically anything under or over the sun. And relationship in concrete situations is rarely if ever found between only two terms; there is usually bewildering multiplicity of relationship, itself a hazard.[9] To clarify, a few examples suffice:

Related things	*Things related to*	*Hazards*
a face formed in the clouds	faces formed of flesh and bones	clouds are only vapor; they vanish quickly; there is a threat to continuance of relationship
the last return of a series of echoes	the shout that was heard	the echo is not a voice; the last return is very faintly heard
the medium of an art	ineffable expressiveness of the work of art	natural recalcitrance of the physical (marble, sound, paint); departure from the mundane in the "ineffable"; the difficulty of seizing ineffability

It is to be noted that the musicologist Leonard Meyer gave prominence to affective hazard in music, using his own terminology but corroborating the idea convincingly.[10] Affective hazard is pivotal to unity of structures. The subordinate elements and norms appeal to a reader's notice. Any precisely achieved effect does. They therefore constitute a threat to the unity that requires ultimate dominance by one. Meanwhile, where several effects are suffused, dominance is gained by the effect of that expression that in the end is found to have sustained the most acute hazard. It causes excitement in proportion to the strength of appeal all the sparring subordinate norms.

At the same time, these subordinate norms help to specify the character of the structure. Frequently, too, hazards are discovered by their being overcome; that is, they are recognized retrospectively as the completed structure is contemplated. The principle that with difficulty has gained dominance is the unifying principle, which gradually endows the work with intelligibility.

Fitness is the principle of unity in what Coleridge called "organic form."[11] The tightness of the unity is cognitively apprehended to be "organic." This is an illusion that arises from reaction to hazard. It *seems* to be cognitive apprehension, but in reality it is affective impulse at the moment when fitnesses or relationships are glimpsed. An aesthetic form is organic when such fitnesses are felt to be triumphs over multiple and various hazards.[12] The response to it is dynamic: the reader continues to discover coherence.

Fitness is grounded in the nature of things. The nature of anything comprises not only its actuality but also its potency—that is, its propensities. And the correspondence between a particular actuality and its potency is necessary, not contingent.[13] When we know what a thing is, we have an idea of its propensities, and we have expectancies. Affectivity is acute in response to relationship in an aesthetic structure finally actualized, if the state of potency has been prolonged, or experienced as suspense. In such a case, as expectancy is met, the awaited terminus seems to occur with an eager initiative of its own. But this is an illusion: the eagerness is in the receiver. The receiver's cognitive grasp of it is suffused with excitement that attends intuition of hazards overcome. The affective impulse is mistaken for depth of cognition of relationship. The resulting union is inviolable and tight, seemingly organic. The more hazardous the term has been, the more it continues to generate meaning. This is because the stimulated mind sees relationship readily.

In poetic tension, there is rivalry of relatabilities, felt fitnesses, or expectancies, for the mind's attention. The resolution of tension by the merest final occurrence of a word is vibrant with meaning. In a plot (dynamic reference), in which meaning occurs in linear sequence of cause and effect, hazards occur in the pull between what seems caused and what results, or, between different possibilities. On the other hand, when reference in a lyric tends in all directions at once, after a glimpse of unifying dominance, the lures of the subordinated expectancies are felt to be distilled as intensity of meaning.

Early in the eighteenth century Alexander Pope anticipated insight into hazard in the poetic process.[14] And in recent years, not only has David Miall *noticed* it in response to music, painting, and poetry, but he explains it. On the basis of neurophysiologists' findings, he has suggested that the frontal cortex of the brain is equipped to enable the function of expectancy. "Unity," he said, " 'grows' out of the various parts," since these create a sense of unity and project or anticipate this unity. He claimed, moreover, that there are links between the frontal cortex and the subcortical structures including the hypothalamus, which constitute "the seat of the emotions." He also quoted with approval French's observation that the behavioral role of the dorsolateral anterior frontal cortex "can be . . . described in the language of association."[15]

It must not be concluded that the elements themselves determine the structure. The linguistic elements of a poem's sound and meaning are organized according to an aesthetic principle. This is what distinguishes poetry from rhetoric whose organizing principle is communicative efficacy and from philosophical or scientific discourse whose organizing principle is logic.

The aesthetic value of a literary work is primary and indispensable. The work will have its own diverse values to the degree that the aesthetic has the primacy.[16] Moreover, the aesthetic is the only kind of value of which this can be said. It is because Shakespeare, Sophocles, Homer, and Chaucer exercised good management of aesthetic structures that critics, professors, students, and readers, "exclusively for pleasure," can so often trace the psychology, the politics, the philosophical implications, and the humor. Effectual aesthetic structures occasion the other various values.

It helps considerably not only to know that the aesthetic value is indispensable to literature but also to know what it is. Different kinds (genres) of literature—of antiquity, the Middle Ages, the Renaissance, and the remote and proximate decades of modern times—have their different proper aesthetic values. It is true, there is no one answer to the question of which qualities observable in structures can be called *aesthetic*. But authors for centuries have recognized that there are such qualities in structure and many still support the position.

5
Aesthetic Values in Literature

AESTHETIC structures characterize great epics (the "sublime," "majesty"), tragedy (the "tragic"), comedy (the "comic"), lyric ("beauty," "grace"), satire ("irony"), and the novel and short story (all or any of these).[1]

The Sublime

Nobody reads epics in the twentieth century except literature majors, and in many instances they read "books one and two for Monday" and "books three and four for Thursday," and so on. When epics were the most accepted type of literature, adults sat for hours, inflamed by the development of imagined events as the torrential language poured fourth. The meaning never reached intensity near the beginning. It was always brought gradually to that point or to those points. The effort of the poet was directed toward managing the sequence of incidents in such a way as to "build up" to peaks of intensity. Such moments have been described as "sublime,"[2] and the condition of affairs at such a moment rewards analysis.

Students still find Longinus's On the Sublime stimulating and modern; sublimity appealed in his own day to Immanuel Kant, and before him to Samuel Johnson, Addison, Pope, and Pope's antagonist, John Dennis.[3] Much further back, in the thirteenth century, Aquinas had observed with approval Aristotle's remark that "we have greater desire for even a little knowledge of noble and exalted things, than even for a conjectural and probable sort of knowledge of inferior things."[4]

It would seem that in the very nature of that which we call the "sublime" there is something that appeals directly to us as people, no matter what century we live in. We sense that to go from the sublime to the ridiculous is to lose scope. And since the sublime is not the graceful, and not elegance, the word *sublime* has its own linguistic independence.

Sublime denotes a quality of meaning. Even when language is found such as that in the *Iliad* or *King Lear* or *Paradise Lost*—language organized in the grand style—sublimity seems localized in the meaning. Actually, the sound and the meaning are not separate except in the mind that abstracts them momentarily for analysis. The lines are heard or read, and they evoke response.

The reader comes to a sublime occurrence with some previous preparation that is important to the response. Whether or not the preparation has been deliberate, it is a fact that the reader is capable to some degree of a certain expectation depending upon his or her total knowledge, familiarity with norms, and past experiences. The reader is in some integrated state mentally.

It is a fact that a sublime occurrence is real. Something is seen, or happens, or is experienced, whether it be Bréton's "objective hazard"[5] or an acute occurrence of meaning in King Lear. Even if, in the mind of a person lying still with closed eyes and deaf ears, the sublime were experienced, it could be said that something occurred in the mind that changed it from whatever it had been before. There would have been a shift in certain relationships. Expression is a possible word for the sublime, whether one is thinking of the cosmos (for the sublime occurs in nature also), or the expression that is the actualization of structure in King Lear, or an expression that remains immanent, simply a realization of sublimity.

There is an expression and there is a receiver, and for the sublime occurrence a condition is presupposed in each. In the expression there is a relation between the actual on the one hand, and the frontiers of what is possible on the other. In the receiver, there is an expectation sanctioned by rule and past experience, and also an intuition that the demands upon expression will be too great in this case. The frontiers of the possible are too wide. Or, in familiar terms, unspoken meaning is too deep for words. Thus, in a sublime occurrence,

$$
\underbrace{
\begin{array}{c}
\text{relations in the expression,} \\[1ex]
\textit{namely} \\[1ex]
\left.\begin{array}{c}\text{the boundary of the actual}\end{array}\right\} \text{to} \left\{\begin{array}{c}\text{the frontiers of the potential}\end{array}\right.
\end{array}
}
\quad
\begin{array}{c}\text{are related to}\end{array}
\quad
\underbrace{
\begin{array}{c}
\text{relations in the receiver,} \\[1ex]
\textit{namely,} \\[1ex]
\left.\begin{array}{c}\text{expectation sanctioned by rule and experience}\end{array}\right\} \text{to} \left\{\begin{array}{c}\text{intuition that demands on expression here are too great.}\end{array}\right.
\end{array}
}
$$

When the sublime is actually occurring, the essential relationship is that between the first and the fourth columns, the boundary of the actual *and* the intuition that demands upon expression are too great in this case. These two factors are related in powerful disequilibrium. What is sensed is that the meaning is growing greater and inundating the mind, which is losing control of it, whereas expression (the actual) is recoiling. Thus the essential structure of the relation of the sublime is that

the boundary of the actual narrows; the actual seems to tend toward annihilation, } it is so exceeded by { the demands upon expression by the growing meaning.

Nowadays, the Surrealist receiver of "objective hazard," like the traditional listener to the *Iliad*, wants to experience something that can be described in the above terms. However, the Surrealist seeks to have an experience more complete in its violence than that furnished by the traditional sublime occurrence described by Longinus. What Longinus wrote was a treatise for rhetoricians on the grand style. The term *sublime* is no longer widely accepted, but the sublime experience is as sought after as it ever was.

The late French theorist Raymond Bayer, making an attempt to distinguish the sublime from the graceful and the beautiful, showed that certain important structures and fixed relations are to be noticed wherever the sublime is encountered. He observed that in the condition called sublime, a perceiving mind discovers a structure that has progressed through alternating phases in a series so rapidly traversed as to be practically simultaneous.[6] Because the phases of advancement are perceived as simultaneous, it violates the reality to enumerate the stages in a series. But provided we bear in mind that all the phases occur in an instant, we know the reality better if we know what the stages are. A clear case can be found in the references to the last lines of Keats's sonnet on Chapman's Homer, which is about the poet's experience of the sublime.

Keats had often had aesthetic experience—had "travelled through realms of gold"—that is, he had read widely the works of the poets; he had seen "goodly states and kingdoms" held by "bards" in "fealty to Apollo." But he reached the acme of the experience when he heard "deep-browed Homer" speak out "loud and bold" in the grand style of the epic. Then something unspeakable occurred. He could not explain it. Words failed. So he resorted to the device of comparing himself to other people whom words had failed.

The poet Keats felt like some "lone watcher of the skies / When a new planet swims into his ken." The primitive grandeur of the night sky is sublime. An astronomer or lone watcher has had experience of its vastness, and is dedicated to a life of exploring it. He looks through the telescope at the familiar vast fields of space between stars, measurable by the positions of the familiar distant stars. This is *equilibrium in structure*, manifold relation of known stars in space. By equilibrium I mean a condition of adjustment of internal relation that occurs when relation is made or found actual. The boundary of the actual is perceived. At this stage, when the structure is in equilibrium, the watcher experiences satisfaction at seeing the immense fields.

Then the astronomer adjusts the lens for outer distance, for more remote fields. The sheer immensity of these mildly startles him into a sense of isolation. He anxiously peers to find the outermost pricks of light, realizing that it takes thousands of years for the light to reach the earth, even traveling at the rate of 186,000 miles per second. The vastness of outer space seizes him. He is visited by the sense of the superhuman, the rarefaction of the actual, and his response is one of tension, and anxiety, and undefined expectancy. The structure is in disequilibrium now; relation is not made actual, but rather, at this moment of rarefaction, relation is still only in the realm of the potential. In the watcher, there is expectation mingled with anxiety.

Then he thinks he is "seeing things." In his solitude and silence, when the astronomers of the past are not by to share, almost with the air of chance without fanfare or warning, a new planet "swims" into view, says Keats. New relationship is actualized, the structure has achieved a new equilibrium, and the astronomer experiences the excitement of surprised response to magnitude of relation on a very large scale. He is "out of the body" with excitement, as his "ken" becomes realization, estimating with the swiftness of the impulse of exhilaration what *that* space must be, and what it implies of other unknown space almost unimaginable. It is as if to say, "This is nothing. We have not even begun." In other words, in the *structure* the actual seems to recoil, as in the *viewer* the presentiment of the magnitude of the potential is enormously enlarged. The astronomer's imagination is staggered and impotent and the emotion of hazard inundates him.

Or, Keats continues, when he first read Homer he felt like the stout-hearted explorer who "with eagle eye" first stared at the Pacific. This time a whole crew of men, not one "lone watcher" but all, on the instant, were frozen to silence, looking at each other "with a wild surmise"—*Wild*, because the unprecedentedness of the moment isolated them as mad men are isolated, unable to share their experience with other men; *surmise*, because they were held by a question, seeming so impossible and yet actual, pointing to so much that was not measurable.

From the example it appears that the question of adjustment in the structure of the sublime is (1) equilibrium when relationship is made actual, (2) disequilibrium in the rarefaction of the actual, (3) a new and vaster equilibrium, followed by (4) extreme rarefaction of actual reference and only potential equilibrium. The receiver experiences satisfaction, then expectation mingled with anxiety, then excited surprise in response to the new equilibrium of unexpected magnitude, followed by intuitive presentiment of increasing magnitude of the growing inadequacy of the actual.

In the last phase, a moment of maximum accumulation of experience, we have what is called the sublime. It is an aesthetic quality that comes as a climax of a progression through phases of structural equilibrium, disequilibrium, more profound equilibrium, disequilibrium, and so on. It depends upon a relation between the boundary supplied by the actual appearance of the star, or of the Pacific, on the one hand, and the receiver's persentiment of unknown vaster universes, or of unknown expanses of ocean, on the other; the experience of the sublime occurs at the instant when the receiver's presentiment is on the increase, and when the actual, although itself enormous, seems in advancement toward annihilation.

The idea that hostility and terror are ingredients of the sublime was popular in the eighteenth century, but it has been frowned upon in the twentieth.[7] Bayer, though, observed that the sublime in the ocean's force does not appear when we find the force to be great, but at the moment when we suspect it is unleashed;[8] and in this he seems to have supported the older idea. I find it convenient, however, to use the word *tragic* for that which produces terror, and *majesty* for the combination of vastness and equilibrium.

In Homer, the meaning was organized analogously, as Keats's simile suggests. The epic is the genre in which the sublime appears clearly. Dostoevsky's Myshkin said that men of former days, Napoleon's days, do not seem to have been "the same people that we are now; it was not the same race as now; in our

age, really it seems we are a different species. . . . In those days
they were men of one idea, but now we are more nervous, more
developed, more sensitive, men capable of two or three ideas at
once. . . . Modern men are broader-minded—I swear that this
prevents their being so all-of-a-piece as they were in those
days."[9]

Whether Myshkin's observation was right about actual men of
former days, the fictional heroes of epic do come to mind when
we think of men "of one idea . . . all-of-a-piece." The epic hero is
"greater than we" as Aristotle said, greater than men usually
are.[10] He is related by his office to the most remote and even the
most humble dwellers of the kingdom, and to the gods of distant
Olympus. He traverses great distances—to Ithaca, to Heorot over
the whale-road, to under-ocean caverns, to Hades. Longinus
mentions Homer's technique in making the vastness of the world
the measure of the leap of horses.[11] Spatial magnitude seems to
heighten the hero's importance.

The hero is further dignified by affective hazard. When a long
time elapses between moment and moment, or term and term,
time is felt to be an obstacle to the relation of the terms, a hazard.
The epic hero is in a path of relation with past ages by ancient
prophecy, by deep-rooted genealogy, and by the whole history of
the nation with which he is intimately identified. He is linked
with the distant future by foreglimpses of prophetic utterance.
Between the youth and a moment of prophecy out of the past, a
vast temporal hazard exists, with all the attendant chances of
mutability. The intervening time is annihilated when the youth
unwittingly fulfills the ancient prophecy, or some vague national
expectation. Time, according to Aristotle, is the measure of motion and of being moved;[12] all that lived and all that happened
(that moved and was moved) between 10,000 B.C. and the fifth
century B.C. did live and did happen, and vast changes duly took
place. This is what imagination stores up instantaneously, and
when the two terms—the moment out of the past and the moment of the youth's unwitting act—are seen to be related, the
ancient moment is heavily charged, and the present moment
freighted by hazard and therefore with affectivity. Both moments
are intensely clear. It is in the imagination of the receiver that
their relation, some crucial reinforcement, is recognized, and
excitement occurs. The epic, in fact, is always of events in geardagum (long ago) as the author of Beowulf says.[13] Temporal
hazard heightens the whole thing. Pope, in the preface to the
Iliad, says, "When we read Homer, we ought to reflect that we are

reading the *most ancient* author in the heathen world; and those who consider him in this light, will double their pleasure."[14]

The epic hero is solemnized also by affective numerical hazard when he is singled out of a nation to perform an act. The imagination immediately stores up, without analyzing, the thousands who were excluded in the choice of these men—Milton's Adam, Achilles, Aeneas, Sohrab, Beowulf. The vast number constitutes a hazard, the chances against the hero's being so singled out. Again, the whole epic is enlarged by the plural voice uttering it or sometimes by the universal voice of the muse. Armies, smoke rising from a hundred altars of sacrifice, a catalogue of ships, hosts of angels, all contribute affectivity.

Affective hierarchical hazards add to the significance of the hero too. The epic character is a king, or a king's son, or the father of the race. Over all the priorities of graded divinities and of past generations of men, he is noticed by Olympus. He is a man of destiny, by the predilection of the father of the gods, or by the eternal decree of Necessity, or by *Wyrd* in *Beowulf*.[15] He is, as an individual, important.

By the disparity between his unique personal nature and ours, by his being "greater than we,"[16] he is enhanced in our eyes. Whereas we are timorous, he is a lion of courage. Beowulf's *mundgripe* has the strength of the grip of twenty men. Achilles' anger is greater than our anger, his grief greater than our grief, his friendship more complete and constant than ours. Whereas we resort to the minor compensations of comfort, the hero, by nature, overleaps the comforts and considerations of the here and now in the interest of a greater and more remote dedication. By the aptness of his wit too, he is felt to be an unusual person; his hearers know him to be endowed by nature with gifts of expression and manner, and he captures all.

The art of the epic is directed to the creating of enormous meaning, so forcible, as Pope said of the *Iliad*, that "no man of a true poetical spirit is master of himself while he reads. . . . Everything moves, everything lives, and is put in action. . . . The reader is hurry'd out of himself."[17]

The language is heightened and extraordinary, the style suited to the speech of gods and heroes. There is considerable difference between the magnitude and force of meaning in the language of the grand style and the style of normal speech which the grand style implies. Taking the elevated style as one term and the normal as the other, the disparity is a hazard. Thus the grand style is in itself charged with affectivity so potent to the poet

Horace that he considered the grand style to be the *differentia* of poetry.[18] It is so arranged that the "sentiment swells and fills out the diction which rises with it," said Pope.[19] The meaning seems to be greater than words can manage.

Figures of speech are large in their scope, just in the correspondence of what present-day critics call the vehicle and tenor. The epic simile draws out the lengthening vehicle and the reader's mind pursues the alternative in the lengthening tenor. Such similes are plentiful in all great epics and familiar to students of English who have read *Paradise Lost* or Arnold's *Sohrab and Rustum*. Milton, like Homer, compounds them and even borrows to advantage. He borrows a famous comparison of the warriors in the *Iliad* pouring out of the side of a ship and scattering to their various tasks, likened to bees pouring out of the hive and descending on the meadows. In Milton's ending of the first book of *Paradise Lost*, the multitude of angels who have defied God and been banished, are flocking to a council:

>   . . . they anon
> With hundreds and with thousands trooping came
> Attended. All access was thronged, the gates
> And porches wide, but chief the spacious hall
>
> . . . .
>
> Thick swarmed, both on the ground and in the air,
> Brushed with the hiss of rustling wings. As bees
> In springtime, when the sun of Taurus rides,
> Pour forth their populous youth about the hive
> In clusters; they among fresh dews and flowers
> Fly to and fro, or on the smoothed plank,
> The suburb of their straw-built citadel,
> New ribbed with balm, expatiate and confer
> Their state-affairs; so thick the airy crowd
> Swarmed and were straitened. . . .

The vehicle in each case is the swarming of bees. The tenor in the *Iliad* is the soldiers pouring out of the ship's hold, and in *Paradise Lost*, the damned spirits flying to the hall.

Bold hyperboles widen the fields of meaning. In hyperbole, the vehicle is greater than the reader's expectation warrants. The vehicle already specifies the direction of imagination, and hyperbole effects in addition an instantaneous enlargement of the meaning range in that direction. There is a fitness too, discovered between vehicle and tenor, although they refer to things of different natures. The hazard in numerous figures of comparison is thus assimilated and the imagination rushes ahead to greater meaning under the affective stimulus. And in the stress of action strained to the utmost, the poet generalizes vehicles to imitate haste.

In the broad fields of meaning, as curious episodes occur, digressing from the main progress temporarily, they might, as in the Odyssey, effect leisureliness and vastness of scale, coming back eventually like tributaries into the larger movement of the "plot."

When the form is gracefully expressed in the grand style, sublimity in the meaning is at its peak. For although the aesthetic structures of grace and of the sublime are direct opposites,[20] it does happen that grace can characterize form that expresses sublime meaning. In such a case, grace seems localized in the process of the expression as a supreme effectualness, felt when the thing appears to be done with ease. True, it is in the response to the meaning that the rarefaction of power is felt; but this happens in proportion as the form is expresed with maximum efficiency, or ease, or with what amounts to astonishing fitness, or grace.

In the big frame of the epic, whether twenty-four or twelve books, whether dactyllic hexameter or Miltonic blank verse or the pause-breached line of Beowulf, the sublime is deliberately attempted. The meaning must seem even bigger than the frame. It must swell the form, so to speak. The mind goes to the words' denotations, thence to connotations and further, and when the images are heaped up with subtle imitation of haste, the impression is that of excitement in the presence of meaning too big to be contained, and of a straining on the part of the form to contain it. The mind does not have leisure to attend to the detail that it glimpses in its rapid passing, because the quick succession of images is drawing it everywhere at once. It sees much and suspects more than it has time to explore. The total effect of this rapid succession is the implication of the form's predicament as if it were to say, "There is too much, let me mean, let me mean, I cannot mean all of it." And this is an expression of sublimity— vast extremity of meaning to be expressed. The force of its magnitude is suspected and left unexpressed, and so meaning is felt to be increasingly greater than the expression that is straining after it.

Sensing the disequilibrium or dynamic nature of this sublimity, the imagination of the receiver looks from term to term, or toward the direction of terms it cannot seize. The poet's art effects this, and Pope described such a moment:

The comparison . . . of a fire which runs thro' the corn and blazes to heaven had exprest at once the dazzling of their arms and the swiftness of their march. After which Homer having mentioned the sound of their feet, superadds another simile, which comprehends both the idea of the brightness and the noise; for here . . . The earth appears to burn and groan at the same time. Indeed, the first of these similes is so full and noble, that it scarce seem'd possible to be exceeded by any image drawn from nature. But Homer to raise it yet higher, has gone into the marvelous, and given it a prodigious and supernatural prospect, and brought down Jupiter himself, array'd in all his terrors, to discharge his lightnings and thunders on Typhoeus. The poet breaks out into this description with an air of enthusiasm, which greatly heightens the image in general, while it seems to transport him beyond the limits of exact comparison.[21]

It is always in the epic *form* that the dynamism is generated: in the dramatic back-and-forth of heroes' speeches, in lively transitions controlled in the tone, in the steady movement of the plot, in the metric structure of "numbers" that "roll along as a plentiful river, always in action, and always full, . . . a tide, the most rapid, and yet the most smooth imaginable."[22]

The form of the epic is complex, as complex as life can be, since "life" is referred to by the shaping meanings. The form is as subtle and ambiguous as sound can be in the prosodic structure, and as hazardous and unique as expression can be in the union of words and what they are to express. To add to the fragility of the form, the successful manipulation of all hazards waits upon words. In the reading of the poetic language of Homer, when a word is occurring, the word before it is no longer heard, and is presently gone from the memory; but the next is then heard, and the next, so that all the sound is rising and passing, occasionally echoing the meaning in patterns of qualitative and quantitative sound. And while this happens, meaning is "leaping," as Pope said.[23] At the sound of the words, imagination apprehends meaning and leaps from the expressed term to the unexpressed, and is lured back by the intensity of the meaning of the next rising expression, which in turn it delightedly pursues, but cannot exhaust before the next, and so forth.

In form that is shaped as a flow of sound against silence in time, and is at the same time referring to space, relation is fleeting and momentary, attended by hazards. *Obstacles to meaning are increased by the lure of sound.* Yet the words denote vehicles of figures; a vehicle calls up the tenor as well as its own peculiar connotations, and these connotations, astonishingly related, drive the imagination further, having specified the direction, from term to term. And thus, *distractions from structure of sound are increased by the demands of meaning.*

The imagination follows from meaning to meaning, seeing relations that flash across hazards, and experiencing the tensions. The lengthening, broadening, deepening paths of connotation beckon the mind and, at the same time, the path of sound of words actually recorded allure the ear. Neither sound nor meaning is relinquished. And when the sound "seems" to "echo" the meaning,[24] the intimacy of the agreement surprises the reader (listener), who has found the actual and is secure, whose mind instantly draws an *inference of spectacular control of meaning,* hence trust in the genius of the poet. The reader is ready to launch out on the meaning.

The unit of the next hexameter line, then the next unit of the next hexameter line, then the next, provides a leisurely harmony, always changing but always keeping the meter. This is beautiful in itself and has its own internal hazards. But the stern meaning of the *Iliad* proceeds, the action growing urgent, the structure scaffolded by vehicle after vehicle of metaphor, deed after deed, words following from deeds, fury following from words, and battle threatening from intensifying fury. It is meaning the mind is after, language straining to overcome its own hazards. Connotations of continuing lines threaten to diminish the mind's hold on the actual reference and to widen it into the unmapped universe of potential meaning.

At such a moment we may again notice that the sound is imitating the meaning; it has triumphed over every hazard, and again actual expression wins momentarily. The meaning never completely actualizes but is come upon as if accidentally as the hexameters unfold. By a swift affective impulse of the imagination, meaning frontiers are widened, and the mind *has not leisure to measure these,* so a new and radical multiplication of affectivity is felt. Although the movement toward ultimate meaning is real, it is only hinted at. And, as Plato said, all the unactualized meaning, in which orbits of extreme hazard occasion affectivity, "drives the soul."[25] The reader has a glimpse in a passing moment of what *seems* like an instantaneous insight into the meaning of all things, a mysterious and profound intuition;

and this triumph is felt with a sudden overwhelming rush, a "wild surmise," to borrow Keats' words. It must be realized, moveover, that when epics were recited (as when they originated),[26] the listeners felt themselves to be close to the heroes and inhabiting a somewhat exposed land. Their awe of the gods could have been more than literary. Besides, they listened for extended periods, experiencing the dynamism of the meaning.

Even in the most solemn phases of the traditional epics of Homer and Virgil there is majesty and celebration. Not only are they old, but they express values, aesthetic and otherwise, of subsequent literary genres. The kinds of literature are not fashioned by the use of hidebound rules; they are based on family resemblances with historical foundations.

Homer, a practicing oral poet, was one of many singers of his day who built narratives on themes and oral traditions. Audiences who listened were as much a part of the traditions as the singers were. A singer would take popular themes leading naturally from one to another to form an integrated song. Some themes had a semi-independent life of their own.

The traditional narratives were serious. Many scholars conjecture that they began as religious, and that the epithets (ox-eyed Hera, bright-eyed Athene) describing deities might have referred to their epiphanies and could have been used to give force to religious invocation.

A singer built his performance on a stable narrative skeleton that he had formed and did not change it except for occasional words. Many readers of our day claim that Homer's epics, so brilliant in diction, prosody, and rhetorical finesse, could not possibly have been orally composed. Professor Lord's study shows rather convincingly how they could have been. He said that epics based on oral traditions are orally composed even now in some countries, notably in Yugoslavia.[27] Homer's poems, he claims, although orally composed and performed, were dictated and written down at a particular time of unknown date. Once written down they were not changed.[28] Some subsequent epics originated as written literature (the *Aeneid*, *Paradise Lost*, and probably others), but *Beowulf* may have been orally composed and was performed with harp accompaniment.[29] Other Anglo-Saxon and even Middle English alliterative poetry is thought to have originated in oral performance.

Although epics had plots, that is, dynamic reference, the outcome of the narrated struggle was known in advance. Therefore, ignorance and mere conjecture were not the basis of suspense, but expectancy and exhilaration. Furthermore, although every part is treated at length, observed Aristotle, the action of an epic has unity.[30] All of the aesthetic values, with the possible exception of the comic, characterize one or another phase of epic. Occurrences of beauty, majesty, grace, and irony are frequent, but the structure as a whole expresses the sublime.

In antiquity, Homer's poetry was also "useful" for history, arts and sciences, and pedagogy. Thus it had both utilitarian and aesthetic values. Other kinds of literature can also have both, since the need or interest of one who values has a bearing on value.

The Tragic

The tragic, although akin to the sublime, has more darkness and madness. The form of tragedy is more restrictive than that of the epic. The sum of all the words is less. Accordingly, the tragic poet does not delay in presenting to our imagination some compelling relation of the protagonist to a unique and lonely destiny.

To be an individual person is to maintain unique basic proportions of character in all circumstances. The dissimilarity separating persons is always implied. The common factor that brings about relation between them is glimpsed now and then, and occasions affectivity. The orbit between character and character gives internal perspective within the frame of characters. But the tragic hero is felt to be related also to the remote and unseen, as is the epic hero. He too is "greater than we,"[31] and thus represents a departure from the normal.

However, he is more alone than the epic hero. Trouble and hostility are always foreshadowed. In addition, the tragic hero is dependent upon a blind intuition of obligation to the unknown. Olympus is never seen; Oedipus rests his authority upon an answer to the riddle of the sphinx; Hamlet has no guarantee that the ghost is not evil; Macbeth is beset by doubt and scruple. But some vision of himself, some clear assurance that he is the one destined, is suddenly actualized for the tragic protagonist. He responds (at first timorously) to glimpses of the magnitude of his unique existence. Oedipus is proclaimed king; the ghost explains the mission to Hamlet; the weird sisters hint at Macbeth's destiny by titles that suggest their foreknowledge. Presently the hero is driven on swiftly by assurances so unique and evanescent that he would not name them. Oedipus decrees the destruction of the man who is responsible for the curse on Thebes, not heeding the fright in the eyes of the citizens. Macbeth, although trembling, listens to the witches, writes to his wife, and invites the king. *It is the plight of the protagonist to draw enormous inference from the slenderest evidence.*

When a mute hint is given of the magnitude of his mission, the implications of fate, he is impelled to rush toward it, precipitated by his excitement at the glimpse of it, because the enormity of the risk lends impetus to the quest. Oedipus, cozened by the oracle, overleaps the warnings of Teiresias; Macbeth, enchanted by the image of supremacy that his wife forges in his heated imagination, overleaps his conscience. Bullough said, "The exceptional element in the tragic . . . is a consistency of direction, a fervour of ideality, a persistence and a driving force which is far above the capacities of average men."[32]

The poet meanwhile increases the hazards by means of language. Words, meaningful in themselves, old and linked by relation with the whole of civilization, quietly separate from the vague obscurity attending their accustomed use and grow devastatingly concrete. Their denotations seem delicately to have sustained the hazard of nonoccurrence. Enchanted, readers feel themselves engaged with the hero's plight. They watch him manfully relinquish the normal securities of life. Oedipus presses on to find out the fatal truth regardless of caution. Macbeth performs the deed of murdering the king. This is a plunge, blind and alone, into the darkness; the hero is driven by the hunch that something, he knows not what, is there, meant for him.

Up to this point the meaning in tragedy is like the sublime meaning of epic. Achilles has defied Agamemnon; Odysseus rashly defies Poseidon's offspring. But instead of finding the next term, that is, the undeniable reassurance he is plunging headlong toward, the tragic hero is dashed against a wall, so to speak, stunned by a stern denial. The term does not exist. The double-tongued oracle gradually appears to have tricked Oedipus. The weird sisters' ambiguity shows itself in Macduff's words, and realization beats brutally at the awakening mind of Macbeth. Whereas the gods were on the side of the epic hero, the tragic hero has been mistaken. He stubbornly pursues the false course, although the *rarefaction of reassurance has now become grim and hostile.* He is freshly stunned by the frown of the god. What presently appears, instead of fulfilling his anticipation, negates it. All the violence of the pursuit that had resulted from the hazard now turns back upon him. Oedipus knows who he is; Macbeth in death combat with Macduff, now knows him to be his destined slayer. *The magnitude of the whole meaning, now negative, hurls itself upon the tragic hero and destroys him.*

The distinction between the tragic and epic hero can be illustrated in diagram. The arrows indicate the drive of the hero's thoughts:

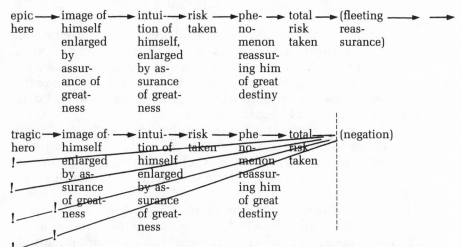

The hero in each case, given some hint of the remote term (an intuition of his greatness), is exhilarated. He himself has become receiver of meaning, that of his own case. He is stirred because the hazard is real and unprecedented. His stimulated imagination leaps to a more hazardously remote terms, finding in it some fleeting reassurance (ὕβρις: *hybris*), and, maddened by urgency, he is beckoned by a unique destiny.

In the case of the tragic, the precipitancy of the hero toward an increasingly lonely destiny is very violent because the hazards are extreme, the reassuring sign from Olympus being perilously slight. The increasing madness drives the tragic hero to blindly conjure up a fatal mirage of unique responsibility. A terrible and electrifying insight into the possibility of its not being there *shifts* the focus of his gaze toward the immense nothingness.

His leap into the dark was destruction and the magnitude of the retrospective meaning destroys him. Frequently this violence is heightened by the last chance occurring just before the catastrophe; the hero has one last opportunity to retrieve his error or forestall his fate before it is too late, but he rejects it.

We, the audience, see and respond to it with pity and terror.[33] The pity and terror are generated and accumulated by the alternating of suspense and satisfaction, potency and actuality, as the

form is gradually specified. The tragic, like the sublime in traditional art, is built up by a series of exigencies in a dynamism.
Although chaos is experienced in the ultimate destruction of the
hero, or in the flooding of the mind by meaning brought to a state
of climax in epic, it is the efficient ordering of a structure's
elements that effects the experience and occasions its aesthetic
value.

Traditionally, the language of tragedy has been pleasurable,
"sweet," as Aristotle said.[34] This is true of the Greek tragedies
and those of Shakespeare and several of his contemporaries.
Beautiful poetic language seems suitable since it is the language
of the rare moment, of people whose stature is eminent, and who
are in the extremity of human desperation.

Furthermore, tragedy is often said to be more "objective" than
the other genres. What makes it seem so is that its whole dramatic structure is formed by "process reference" (dialogue,
speeches among characters, not the speech of the author directed
to the audience).[35]

The tone in tragedy is serious, often reflective and philosophical. The pressure of calamity is sometimes superhuman, as in
epic. The presence of gods is suggested, not by their appearing,
speaking, or acting, as in epic, but by the relentless fate bearing
down on the protagonist as if by a hostile agency. In Shakespeare
there is occasionally a visitation by a preternatural being (ghosts
and witches were phenomena of interest in his day) whose words
aid in propelling the protagonist toward decision. In Greek tragedy, the lyric choruses sometimes addressed the gods in prayer.

Genres exist as family resemblances, historically based. But
there are differences between one epic and another, between one
tragedy and another. Each literary work is unique. But in all
tragedy there are recognizable features. Ancient tragedy had
come to a peak of excellence with Sophocles, and Aristotle used
his *Oedipus Rex* to exemplify the principles of tragedy in his
Poetics. Subsequently the Romans expressed tragic meaning in
drama. Shakespeare, who probably had knowledge of Aristotle's
Poetics (which was translated into English when Shakespeare
was in his early thirties),[36] was influenced by the Roman Seneca
and by the lives of great men as narrated by Plutarch. His tragedies show all these influences.

He was heir not only to the ancient classical traditions of
tragedy and comedy. He absorbed those of medieval drama, as is
sometimes evident. He had prodigious intelligence and talent for
the tragic and the comic. Several features of tragedy have

changed in the four centuries since Shakespeare, but the tragic is still entrenched in some modern literature and in the novel. Joseph Conrad seems to have favored it since he experimented in combining it with the novel form, at least in *Lord Jim* and especially in *The End of the Tether.*

The Comic

The alternative to characters "greater than we" is those "less than we," which is Aristotle's designation for the comic character.[37]

Between the sublime and the tragic on the one hand, and the comic on the other, there is a difference in what might be called scale. Comic meaning, occurring in the neighborhood of persons "less than we," is uncommonly small in dimension. The smallness is not physical (although it can be) but moral, psychological, and intellectual. Normally we expect people to exhibit a certain amount of response to what is past, such as a promise made or an injunction given or a lesson learned. We expect them to show response to what is present also, and responses would render them significant, dignified, their existence implying, however tacitly, a soul, aspirations, serious things; and their vision of the future would be thoughtful and responsible.

But in the actions of comic characters, the signification is that they are irresponsible, all stomach, all physical appetite or laziness or stupidity. In their acts, the characters are suddenly seen to be precisely in the condition of emerging from the uniqueness that is implied by human personality and the normal obligations of people, into that universal groove of prone human nature that requires least of the soul or spirit. The body, let us say, together with all its demands and predicaments, or sheer vacancy of mind, or distortion of the concept of self, becomes central.

Meaning, which is always actualized by being apprehended, tends to be conditioned by the mind's previous expectancy; and in the comic instance, normalcy is unconsciously assumed. At the precisely comic moment, meaning registers with a shocking foreshortening. The receiver, assuming the normal dimensions of a person, finds this comic character less. In any deviation from the normal the normal is implied. The shock is like that which people going downstairs in a giddy mood of laughter might experience, were the steps shallower than they expected.

Comic characters' shallowness quickly becomes noticeable.

Not related to a serious and remote destiny, they do not overleap the comforts and considerations of the here and now in the interests of some dedication. They do not, as any normal person would, keep their promises or display a sense of responsibility. Therefore, *no affective interest attends our response to them as people.*

A past promise would be one term, the person who made it, now in his or her present situation remembering it, would be the other, and the intervening time and change of circumstance would constitute a hazard, so that supreme fidelity would tend to induce affective response. But comic characters disregard past promises and the remote future, finding only the nearest thing at hand desirable. They are not lonely or isolated, but enmeshed as one of the million, and even their most acute anxieties are about the immediate.

There is a spirit of holiday about the comic, because the remoter things related to a person in normal life are put aside, and imagination is given up to the contemplation of a person foraging in a business-like way for all that he or she can get. There is no pity in the swift this-way-and-that building up of incidents to a climax of irresponsibility and misunderstanding. What this entails for the reader is the rapid perception of terms cognitively received occurring on all sides. There is no terror.

It is true that there are extreme hazards in classical comedy, occasioned by wit and dramatic ironies swiftly seen in retrospect—hazards of tone and of the apparently accidental circumstance that puts a strain on probability. But the affective impulse (enjoyment) from such hazard is felt as applause of the mechanism and enthusiastic surrender to the spirit of the rogue behind the author's conception, not affection for the character. The technique of rapid manipulation of comic occurrence is directed always toward the shrinkage of personality and responsibility.

Is is true, this type of purely comic character comes closer to ancient Greek and especially Roman comedy than to that of the Middle Ages and the Renaissance. The classical flavor was missing in the centuries intervening; medieval drama and narrative arose from totally other origins. The comic in the Middle Ages and Renaissance often had admixtures of other elements noticeable, for instance, in Chaucer's Wife of Bath and Pandarus, and in Shakespeare's Falstaff, Dogberry, and others. Their slyness and wit sometimes gave them the upper hand, so the joke was not always on them. The laughter was sometimes with, not always at, them.[38]

It seems, meanwhile, that viewing the older aesthetic structure in its purity enables one to identify the later admixtures clearly and thus to recognize the ingredients in specific characters and momentary hilarious situations.

The convenience of this appears in the process of considering medieval, Renaissance, and modern literature, in which purely comic characters interact with others that are socially privileged or intelligent but at the same time funny. This is a common phenomenon in Shakespeare's romantic comedies, although less so in Ben Jonson's, where the majority of characters come closer to the classical. Both comic types are richly exemplified in great literature.

The basic distinction between both sublime and tragic meaning on the one hand and purely comic meaning on the other is clear when they are juxtaposed and seen in relation to the normal from which both are departures. In the diagram below, E represents the epic hero, T, the tragic protagonist, N, the normal man, and C, the comic character. The vertical solid line represents *normalcy* of character dimension. The arrows show *achieved* dimension of character. Dotted lines E and T mean *potentiality* for further greatness. The vertical dotted lines suggest the comic character's self-concept, not achieved.

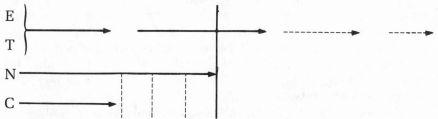

In the hazards of time, space, number, hierarchy, and intrinsic nature the protagonist's obligations to the past, present, and future would be temporal hazards. The purely comic character is without hazards. He fails to keep promises when he finds himself in the neighborhood of a tavern, a pretty girl, or a bribe. He runs from battle, deserts his vixen wife, and turns away from the frowning face of tomorrow. There are no spatial hazards of relatedness to remote borders of the kingdom; he navigates between his own park bench and the tavern, between one street and the next. He is not singled out and important; he is individual but not personal, and consequently he is like everybody in the world, reduced to a common denominator of proneness to human weakness.

Every distinctly human feature, developed by intellectual insight and free choice in action, is dormant and untroublesome.

The comic character has no status, a fact often exploited by the author, who displays him in a debauchery of arrogance in the presence of his fellows. Even though dukes (Senior in *As You Like It*; Theseus in *Midsummer Night's Dream*) are given to merriment and full notice of their clowns, it is in Arden or at wedding festivals, where responsibility is temporarily shut out, and Touchstone or Nick Bottom rules the good-natured nobility for an hour. The natural eminence characteristic of tragic and epic heroes is completely foreign to a purely comic character. His wit is a blunder, his malapropisms are unconscious, and his personal wares are a dime a dozen. The momentum is toward exaggeration.

In the use of hyperbole, the norms of the sublime, the tragic, and the comic are distinguishable. In ancient epic, hyperbole was a fitting device, observable in the management of the marvelous and in boldness of expression. In tragedy, it provided for the extremes of pitiable and fearful meaning, the structuring of which effected a catharsis of emotions and assumed grandeur of expression. On the other hand, hyperbole is one of comedy's chief graces, as Demetrius long ago pointed out.[39] Whereas in epic, it instantaneously distances the meaning's boundary, in comedy it instantaneously shrinks it. In other words, the spirit of hyperbole is to adjust the second of two related terms, and therefore to adjust hazards in the range of meaning. In the tragic and the sublime where the hazards are great, emotion is high; but in comedy where they srhink, emotion does not result. The reader is amused, carefree, and feeling the complete opposite of serious anxiety, pity, or terror.

However, comedy does progress to peaks of intensity. This does not mean that each incident must be bigger and better than the foregoing. Even a structure such as that which La Drière described as a series[40] inevitably comes to such a point at some stage, in some way. When a lively tennis game is played and the gaze of the audience turns now to one side of the net, then to the other, and back again to this side, even although this looks like a pure series of acts always very much the same, by the fifth, sixth, or seventh return of the ball the tension mounts to a high pitch, and the play finally brings a burst of applause. The reason for this is that the audience brings to the spectacle assumptions based on normalcy of endurance. In both tragic and comic structures this phenomenon is frequent. The comic, like the tragic and the sublime, is achieved sometimes by serial and sometimes by systemic structure.

Up to this point, theory has been the central consideration. For prolific readers of literature who, while reading theory constantly apply it to familiar works, the following section on *evaluation* may appear less necessary and less interesting.

However, many people like to be shown. In fact, in the attempt to show aesthetic values in literature I have often been further awakened and more firmly convinced of the presence of value. By exemplification I will show: the comic, in Shakespeare's characterization of Nick Bottom in *Midsummer Night's Dream*; the aesthetic of grace, in Theocritus's pastorals, in an eight-line poem by Frances Cornford, and in Keats's *Ode to Autumn*; beauty as aesthetic value, in Shakespeare's Sonnet 73; the aesthetic structure of comic irony and its appearance, in a section of Chaucer's *Nun's Priest's Tale*, tragic irony, in a short poem by Thomas Hardy; and brute irony, in Hemingway's *The Killers*.

In more recent literature generally, although aesthetic values are frequently and eminently present, they are mixed, less pure. The study of these also is facilitated by insight into the structures of traditional aesthetic values. That the comic of ancient classical comedy was sometimes exemplified as late as Shakespeare is clear.

Nick Bottom is purely comic. It is observable (1) in what he most wants, (2) in the way he sees himself, (3) in the way the unintelligent characters see him, and (4) in the way the intelligent characters see him.

(1) He wants to shine among his peers by bossing them, claiming the center of attention, and airing "knowledge" and oratorical language. He announces his name to the Duke; he hopes to appear gentlemanlike, to originate ideas, to be thought superior, philosophical, and humorous. He is patronizing. He likes to eat, to sleep, to seem brilliant, to draw tears from an audience, and to prolong his moment of glory.

Quince is the director of the rustics' play, but he takes directions and a good bit of supplanting from Nick, not always to the advantage of the performance they are preparing for, but always to Nick's aggrandizement. Nick talks incessantly in malapropisms, offering ruinous suggestions. He blunders unconsciously when rehearsing and is vain about his singing while wearing an ass' head. He is unctious and polite to Titania's four attendants, but anxious to be scratched, fed, and put to sleep. He roars like an orator in figures of speech.

(2) This is not the way he sees himself. From his didactic air, his grabbing up parts of the play, imagining himself before the

Duke and the ladies, gloating over his own suggestions, making far-fetched jokes and showy observations to Titania's attendants, by name-dropping and offering an epilogue to his audience, he manifestly considers himself superior, capable, original, and knowledgeable. He feels he is indispensable, brilliant, elegant, wise, informed, and even witty. He affects the speech of gentlemen and thinks he can hold the audience captive.

(3) Poor Quince admires him, trusts his judgment, and flatters him until Bottom's energetic display of superiority tires him out, and then he and the others stop reacting—but only for a while. Snout and Starveling momentarily enter into the planning of the play, showing signs of even imitating Nick, as does Quince. Flute puts in a solicitious word for him too. Titania's saccharine praise and love-longing for Nick are the sign that she is still under the practical-joke enchantment wrought by Oberon. Her daintiness and grace are a foil to Nick's grossness and animality. When she embraces him as her "sweet love" his ugliness is magnified. Every thought, longing, and speech is in character. Nick's portrayal, exaggerated as comic characterization often is, is consistent. Especially comic moments are unusually transparent to the reader, and his malapropisms are unusually innocent.

(4) The contrast between Nick's opaqueness in self knowledge and the casual accuracy of Puck's observations about him effects a shrinkage of his personal effectiveness. The remarks of Philostrate and the double-talk of Theseus and the sophisticated courtiers at the play have the same result.

Nick is not a qualitatively changing character. There is no growth, only additional revelation of his limits. He is untroubled by introspection, and his self-complacency is never redeemed.

The comic grows to rare intensity at times, for instance, when Nick, in ignorance of his transformation, yells at Snout, who is staring at him in terror, "You see an ass-head of your own, do you!" Insult is added to injury (unfelt) when Hippolyta's soft-spoken words break the silence: "Beshrew my heart but I pity the man." The strain on probability, Nick's intellectual and psychological smallness betrayed by his mistaken concept of himself, his debauchery and arrogance in the presence of his fellows—all characterize him as comic. Puck accurately sums him up as "the shallowest thickskin of them all." *Shallow* being the opposite of *bottomless*, Shakespeare aptly named him Bottom.

Generally, unlike the tragic and especially unlike the wide-ranging sublime meaning of epic, on a larger-than-life scale, the comic causes a sudden rebound. Hazards are not in magnitude but in the mechanisms of actualization of meaning. The comic response is sometimes labelled intellectual. However, both the sublime and the comic are conditions of meaning structure, distinct from reality more often than not. The difference is that whereas *affective* meaning in epic registers first and continues to expand, *cognitive* meaning in comedy registers quickly and sometimes explosively, and the savor of left-over normal meaning is experienced as a contrast that shifts the tone.

The Graceful

In literature, past and present, the clumsiness of the comic is contrasted with the efficiency of the graceful. The latter is found in a wider range of both reality and literary structure and is less easy to trace. Grace, as I have noted elsewhere, is mentioned in Homer, in the early classical and the later Alexandrian period of Greek literature,. in the Roman Golden Age and the so-called Silver Age, and in European countries from the early Renaissance through the subsequent centuries. It has been ascribed to both nature and art.[41]

Although grace is commonly noticed in dance and in other movement, its presence has been observed also in fixed and motionless things such as ancient earrings, cups, architecture, sculpture, paintings, posture, drapery, trees, flowers, and any number of visible and audible structures.[42] The word is used sometimes to describe wit, manners, and oratory. For a few centuries grace was called the *je-ne-sais-quoi* because, although it is acutely experienced, it is delicate and obscure.[43] However, because it has been prominent in literature from antiquity on, I shall attempt to explain it, then to summarize it in a definition, and then to suggest a brief and effectual method of identifying its appearance.

Grace that characterizes physical movement such as dance, as well as the grace of immobile objects, and the grace of wit, manner, and oratory, although it seems to be inhabiting three different realms, is nevertheless traceable to the same causes. No matter where it appears it has the same aesthetic structure.

Raymond Bayer, who published a two-volume study of grace, first recognized several features of it in slow-motion pictures of a seagull as it left the ground, mounted in the air, and coasted in curved arcs. As the bird was lifting itself off the ground, it was ugly; its wings, neck, feet, and jerking movements betrayed strain and difficulty. Once it began winging its way upward, the strength of its wings in regularity of upward and downward motion seemed forceful and seemed to be gaining ease at the same time. There was an appearance of success, and then "ease," in the splendid command of the direction of curves. The gull had complete control of the counterforces of gravity and wind. *Grace is always the result of a precise ratio of force and counterforces,* Bayer concluded.[44] We do not see forces, we see the expression, the effect of them.

Bayer made a further discovery when he took pictures of an athlete in a very high leap. Although it was spectacular, crowned with success, it was not graceful. The athlete's successive movements, the bulge of his muscles, and the straining to achieve were visible. There was great force in his strength, but the struggle to overcome the counterforces of gravity, magnitude of distance, and pressure of air, was ungraceful. However, when he wore a loose tunic over the shorts he had worn at first, thus concealing the features that showed strain, the result was supremely graceful. The effects of the counterforces were invisible, although intuited. The delicateness of the ratio between the force and the counterforces was extreme, at the moment when grace was acutely experienced. The movement *seemed* contingent, unexpected, appearing casually as if by chance. The force triumphing over the hidden counterforces caused the appearance of contingency in the externalization of the expression.

To say that the ratio between the force and the counterforces is delicate in the extreme is to say that the counterforces are intuited to be almost too great for the force to triumph over them, to express itself. The counterforces are felt to be a hazard or obstacle to the triumph of the force. We have already seen that the overcoming of intuited hazards causes affectivity. Moreover, in the aesthetic of grace, that the counterforces are concealed and that *ease* is observed in the outward expression causes additional intuition of hazard, of the rareness of such excellence overcoming the ordinary to which we are accustomed. We feel the tensions, expecting effort, and when we register the graceful act or expression, all complications resolve themselves as if by magic. The receiver experiences pleasant excitement. Even though grace is the aesthetic sign of some sort of definite economy, a reality imposes itself upon us. The ratio is of forces that are partly (not entirely) psychological. Grace is an aesthetic value, and the receiver of value in general, the person experiencing the value, is an element of the valuable occurrence. The particular factors in the athlete's graceful leap, which involved the psychological, were intuitions of counterforces or hazards, intuited although their direct signs were invisible. Furthermore, because they were not directly known, the ratio of the forces to the counterforces was only estimated.

However, because the force triumphed over the counterforces, could it not be said that the ratio was known? I say, no, not with any exactness, for the reason that the triumph was accomplished with ease. The intuited counterforces, overcome with ease, resulted in an impulse of affectivity that was caused by a hint of unactualized (leftover) potential.

Because gracefulness involves both an objective appearance (the leap, the bird in flight, the dance) and a subjective psychological occurrence in the receiver or witness to the appearance,[45] an account must be given of each of these if grace is to be understood. We have already seen that in the performance there is a preliminary relation (preliminary not necessarily in time, but a *sine qua non*) between the boundary of the actual and visible and the frontiers of the potential and invisible. And in the receiver too, there is a preliminary relation between sanctioned expectation and intuited presentiment.

But what is the precise relation of grace? Initially it can be said to be a relation between the boundary of the actual manifestation and the unseen intuited frontiers of the potential. But the essential structure of grace is one of dynamic disequilibrium. In the performance, the force exceeds the counterforces, and in the receiver, the actual seems greater than the intuited presentiment, in retrospect. Because it appears to be accomplished with ease, the receiver draws instantaneous inference of superior force unactualized as yet. He or she is surprised, because in his or her mind, the counterforces now seem not to work against, but rather to support, the force. Reason is suspended, the apprehended effect seeming greater than the apprehended cause.

The receiver succumbs to, puts trust in, the sensed superiority of the graceful person or motion or appearance, and experiences affectivity; there is pleasure in witnessing the abandonment of habitual imperatives, that is, the resolving of effort, and in witnessing a profound experience of the immediate. The receiver's admiration of the ease and economy of the agreement or charm brings even a volitional impulse: a new superior imperative, a success, seems to win him. Graceful poems, said Horace, lead the soul of the listener wheresoever they will (*Non satis est pulchra esse poemata: dulcia sunto / et quocumqumque volent animum auditoris agunto*).[46]

The unusually long and widespread history of grace includes its application to gods and goddesses, graces of person and behavior, literary and oratorical style, gardens, the dance, athletics, painting, music, architecture, wit, and so on.[47] But this need not defeat the study of it. What we have seen can be compressed into a definition, and its various manifestations can be accounted for. Practically everyone who has written about it has said that it characterizes a structure of one kind or another.

I have already defined grace elsewhere as "the unerring fitness of a form, great or small, to its own nature, a fitness resulting from the triumph of a force that appears casually without exploiting itself, over hazards intuited but not explicitly defined, the triumph appearing in such a manner as to render the fitness apparently inevitable, economical, easy and natural; and though apparently accidental, yet of so rare an excellence as to appear the perfection of the form's own nature, and thus intimately expressive of its nature."[48]

In order to have insight into a graceful manifestation, whether it be physical movement or the swift sally of intuition, it is necessary to identify (1) the force, (2) the counterforces, and (3) the specific nature or end to which the movement is driving. These three elements are different in *all* manifestations of grace, its occurrences being always unique and contingent. But all other aspects of grace are the same, no matter to what we attribute it. The crucial questions for analysis are aimed therefore at the three enumerated elements.

Suppose, for example, that a bus rider's attention were attracted to a short stray curl at the back of a girl's neck. A thousand frail fibers take the same general direction as they leave her neck, a direction toward making a curvature. Curvature itself is a gradual triumph of centripetal over linear force, effecting in the receiver a gradual progression of intuition from expectancy to pleasurable apprehension.

The point, I repeat, is that although the force, the hazard or counterforces, and the specific end are variable, all other elements of grace are the same. In literature, the nature or end of the particular piece is intuited, imagined without the support of evidence.

In dance, in walking, and even in gesture and design, grace does not present much difficulty because the forces, counterforces, and ends in view are fairly recognizable. But in literature, where forces are not physical or visual, it could pose some problems. Nevertheless, grace has been intimately associated with poetry for over three thousand years. In recent decades commentators on literature have not understood grace well, but it is still in our midst everywhere and in some work of poets who brilliantly exemplify it.

In Homer, the gods bestowed it on men, and grace characterized artistic process. It was explicitly characteristic of the gods—the graces, Aphrodite, Eros, Pallas Athene, and Hermes—also of lesser divinities—Calypso and the nymphs who attended Nausicaa.[49]

In the Odyssey grace characterized also the speech of gifted men who used understatement casually. It was found in sorcery, in music, in love and erotic infatuation, in wit, in poems, and in jewelry and sculpture. It was joyous, associated with modesty and charm, with privilege and giftedness, with beauty and readiness of speech, with kindness and affability, and with seduction.[50]

It attended process that was delicate and subtle, sweet sounding, free, and easy, specifying movement and control. It was incompatible with stupidity, effort, and boastfulness, and compatible with prerogative and cultivation demonstrated by readiness of wit.[51]

Greeks, for centuries after Homer, were educated in schools where they learned, even memorized, his works. By the third century B.C. in Alexandria, Homer was available in books. However, the literary products of that age were un-Homeric in many ways. Alexandria, the metropolis, was large and thronged with strangers. The poets were imbued with epicureanism and feminine prestige at the court. The incentive required to sustain epic was dissipated. However, the arts were applauded and cherished. Sculptors, painters (such as Apelles), tapestry weavers, the numerous jewellers, all desired grace. The poets dwelt on thoughts of the fabulous Homeric land of Phaeacia "abandoned to idleness," of the sunny isle of Calypso, of Circe the sorcerer, and of the "golden" gods—Aphrodite, Eros, the Graces, Hermes, and the nymphs of Nausicaa. The poets emphasized timelessness, the Hours, and the play of graces and loves in eroticism, which was notable in the poetry of Philetas (Theocritus's teacher and friend) to his students. The poets liked wit, which was congenial to leisure and social intercourse.[52]

Echoes of Homer were erudition only. In the new era poets

celebrated the grace of the athletes of Cos (Theocritus's birth-place, to which he returned at the end of his life). The poets were conscious of ancient genres with subjects and processes that expressed grace. Grace became an attribute not of the Homeric hero but of girls and boys. The gods had become decorative symbols of grace. Grace characterized the writing of bucolic pastoral and erotic elegy. It became associated with elegance, slenderness, smallness, and especially subtlety. The poets contrasted it merrily with homely realism.

In time, the dimensions of poetic meaning were minimal, confined to the exigent pleasure of the moment. The sounds were treble, charming but thin, in the "plain style." Grace became the be-all and end-all of poetry, which was felt by Roman Stoics to have lost all seriousness. Three pupils of the elegiac poet Philetas—Herondas, Hermesianax, and Theocritus—became pastoral poets as did Bion and Moschus.

Theocritus was eminently successful in originating what is called "the little song . . . in the country,"[53] and his technique appeared two thousand years later again in an English poem (Keats's "To Autumn"). To conclude this treatment of grace as an aesthetic value, I shall digress on Theocritus's art as exemplification of pastoral.

His poems were called *idylls* (εἰδύλλια, "little pictures") and later pastorals, because some refer to country scenes. However, the history of his work and even the nature of pastoral poetry has become obscure to many scholars. Legrand noted that poems 1, 5, 10, and 15 are dialogues, 2 is a lyric mime, 3, a monologue, 6, 7, 11, and 18 are narrative in part, 13 affects the form of a letter, 7 is a page of personal memoirs, 15 is a "placet" destined to come to the prince's notice, 22 is a hymn, 24, an epyllion, and 15, a mime or dialogue.[54] Obviously Theocritus was not striving for a clear-cut genre. His idylls were widely recognized to have been influenced by Homer and to use Homeric dialect with admixture of Doric; but everywhere they reflect third-century B.C. sophistication, world-weariness, and artistic elegance.

The pastoral made a strong appeal to poets. Roman contemporaries of Theocritus—Tibullus, Catullus, Propertius—under the influence of Philetas, showed similar trends of grace and eroticism in their elegiac poems. In later days, Virgil tried pastoral poetry, and much later, Edmund Spenser and Michael Drayton, Bescari and Tasso, Sir Philip Sidney, Milton, Dryden, Pope, Ambrose Phillips, Shelley, Keats, and Tennyson tried it too. A few of these poets wrote like Theocritus, but most of them did not.

Critics in the past have frequently alluded to pastoral poetry. Clear signs that they were aware of its existence appear in Chaucer's *Hous of Fame* and *The Merchant's Tale*, in Roger Ascham, John Lyly, Shakespeare, and Molière, in courtiers in the court of Louis XIV, and in critical discourses on the pastoral by Fontonelle, Wycherly, Pope, Samuel Johnson, and Ambrose Phillips.

However, Theocritus originated and excelled in it. He lived in Cos, then Sicily, then Alexandria, and then Cos again. In all of these places the graceful was the climate of the arts. He complained of the pragmatism of the age to the Graces, mocked the vulgarity of the *nouveau riche* with rare tact, brought out the daintiness of a nymph by the foil of a cyclops' clumsiness and stupidity, showed the teasing of the monster by Galatea (compare Nick Bottom and Titania), and presented the hyperbole of the youth Hylas ensnaring the god of love himself. Theocritus captures the infinitesimal in a mood of idleness—the wave rolling up on the shore showing the reflection of the dog running on the sand, the dry thistledown on a hot summer day, tossed like the fickle nymph this way and that, never settling.

The slightness and the mood of idleness in themselves express ease. The poet refers (Idyll 7) to vines pruned in summer to let in the October sun. There is tranquil enjoyment of life in the open air; every sense is invaded with the breath of fruits. It seems that the Muses feed the singing shepherd, their utterance issuing from his lips with such sweetness as to attract the bees.

Theocritus frequently induces the mood of timelessness to prepare for the distillation of grace. A nocturnal weaving of a spell by the sorceress Simaetha (Idyll 22) to bring back her lover suggests Lyly's *Endymion*, and more daintily, Shakespeare's *Midsummer Night's Dream*. The contrast between Nick Bottom's awkwardness and Titania's grace is found frequently as a technique in Theocritus: In Idyll 15, the realism of the chatty Syracusan women leaving the crowd to feed their hungry husbands is a foil to the song they had stopped to hear, addressed to Aphrodite, about the Hours (seasons), slowest of goddesses, kind to the desire of mortals. The Hours were the givers of all beauty and fragrance.

The apparent effortless contingency turns into an epitome of grace everywhere in his work. The receiver applauds Theocritus's ease and control. That the poet was expressing grace is clear. Besides, not only does he frequently mention the Graces, gracefulness, and the Hours, but Idyll 16 is entitled *The Graces*. He ends the poem with a brief conclusion, ostensibly artless but

celebrating art. It is about Heracles, who grew to youth under his
mother's authority, and under tutors. His food and clothing were
natural, his tunic "made without art," coming halfway down the
thigh.[55]

I have chosen two poems—a short lyric and a pastoral—to
illustrate the subtlety of grace. The lyric, "The Guitarist Tunes
Up," is by Frances Cornford:

> With what attentive courtesy he bent
> Over his instrument;
> Not as a lordly conqueror who could
> Command both voice and wood,
> But as a man with a loved woman might,
> Inquiring with delight
> What slight essential things she had to say
> Before they started, he and she, to play.

The eight-line poem consists of one sentence, giving the matter
apparent slightness. It is mildly exclamatory, gradually becoming
declarative, hence commonplace and quiet; and it is orderly and
complex, each phrase directed to its own function, as if said with
composure. The semicolon at the end of the second line suggests
completeness, but from there on the sentence is clearly periodic,
moving smoothly and purposefully. The word order is normal
and unnoticeable until the last line, "started . . . to play," is
interrupted by the words "he and she." The words "he and she"
are thus given unusual prominence, and the delay of the words
"to play," while it is like an afterthought, is crucial. The double
meaning of the word "play" opens on its hinge at the same time
that the poem closes quietly. Then individual words become
louder and more noticeable—for instance, "inquiring with delight," which calls up the twin pictures of the courteous lover
and the musician's attentive tuning process. The picture grows
clearer in the witty words, "slight essential things she had to
say," which sum up descriptively the behavior of the woman and
the precision of the preliminary tuning of a guitar.

The reader is pleased by the force of such aptness (the intuited
counterforce being the oddness and the more likely inaccuracy of
the denotation) and does not notice that the movement is
smoothly proceeding toward a compounding of wit in the casual
plain language of the last line. The scale of the simile is tipped
toward love-making of the man and woman, and the playfulness
of the tone is clear; it echoes and redoubles on the backward look
at the title.

Not only are these grammatical, but the rhetorical features are effectual too. There is a sense of ease and inevitability, and an air of privilege about the smooth unshowy management of the meaning. The sense is increased by the invisibility of any speaker or addressee.

The most central, unifying aspect appears at first to be in the aptness of the simile. But one by one, then two or three at a time, aspects of pattern begin to appear, in assonance (attentive/bent) and rhyme (bent/instrument), which reinforces the links in the meanings of the words. Presently one sees that she is his instrument: he inquires always with delight, and when with her he is alive. There is connotative unity in the feudal words, "courtesy," "bent," "lordly," "command." and "loved woman," giving charm and universality to love. The rhymes—bent/instrument, could/would, and might/delight (tied playfully to slight)—are linked in both sound and meaning, as are the alliterated words—conqueror/could/command, woman/wood, man/might, and slight/say). The poet's use of "she" for the guitar reinforces the unity. The music comes alive in the words "They started, he and she, to play" at the same time that the love-making is centralized. The mood of each (music, love) reinforces the other, and the last word echoes and vibrates with the accumulation of meaning. Although the speaker is never referred to, credit accrues to her from the ease and grace of management; unspent reserves are felt and applauded by the reader. It is unsparring and unambitious, but it teases us into looking again, and we feel it to be no common achievement.

The following ode by John Keats, "To Autumn," achieves grace too, in a different way.

Season of mists and mellow fruitfulness,
  Close bosom-friend of the maturing sun;
Conspiring with him how to load and bless
  With fruit the vines that round the thatch-eaves run;
To bend with apples the mossed cottage-trees,
  And fill all fruit with ripeness to the core;
    To swell the gourd, and plump the hazel shells
  With a sweet kernel; to set budding more,
And still more, later flowers for the bees,
Until they think warm days will never cease,
    For Summer has o'erbrimmed their clammy cells.

Who hath not seen these oft amid thy store?
  Sometime whoever seeks abroad may find

Thee sitting careless on a granary floor,
   Thy hair soft-lifted by the winnowing wind;
Or, on a half-reaped furrow sound asleep,
   Drowsed with the fume of poppies, while they hook
      Spares the next swath and all its twinéd flowers:
And sometimes like a gleaner thou dost keep
   Steady thy laden head across a brook;
Or by a cider-press, with patient look,
   Thou watchest the last oozings hours by hours.

Where are the songs of Spring? Aye, where are they?
   Think not of them, thou hast thy music too—
While barred clouds bloom the soft-dying day,
   And touch the stubble-plains with rosy hue;
Then in a wailful choir the small gnats mourn
   Among the river sallows, borne aloft
      Or sinking as the light wind lives or dies;
And full-grown lambs loud bleat from hilly bourn;
   Hedge crickets sing; and now with treble soft
   The redbreast whistles from a garden croft;
      And gathering swallows twitter in the skies.

The grammar of the poem effects the languor and relinquishment of the pastoral—compound words, nonverbs performing
the function of verbs (mossed, plump, drowsed, bloom), and
archaisms in the second and third stanzas. The personification of
autumn, perhaps as an ancient goddess (Ceres for instance),
gathers to a felt presence and then vanishes.

The words have a certain simplicity. Only four have three
syllables, and three of these are present participles. All the rest
are of one or two syllables.

Agency though not expressed is felt by the reader to be personal. The pronoun "him" (line 3) refers to the sun as co-
conspirator "to load and bless," the other conspirator being
autumn with "hair soft-lifted" (line 15). These are only two,
rather muted references to gender.

The progression in the use of the second and third person
shows a clear cessation of the second person in the first stanza,
an interweaving of second and third person in the second stanza,
and a complete fading out of the second person in the last nine
lines of the third stanza. The sequence thus supports the relinquishment of the pastoral, the absence of the second person
suggesting a gathering reverie.

In all three stanzas, nouns are numerous—thirty-four singular
and twenty-two plural. The effect is abundance and variety. And

among the nouns in the singular, seven are abstract and four are collective. Concrete impressions invade the speaker, who becomes increasingly abstracted.

The inducement of reverie by relinquishing the second person after the second line of stanza three (line 24) is noticeable again in the abandoning of personal pronouns at that same line. There is a felt surrender to invading impressions. It is confirmed by the dimming out of all pronouns after that line.

The poem is scaffolded by adjectives throughout, thirty-four of them descriptive, eighteen of these participial as well, and only eleven delimiting. The usage is slow moving, sensuous, and receptive rather than active.

The verbs, thirty in number, could be expected to counteract that impression, but they do not. Not one of them is locomotive, not even "run"; none is strenuous, not even "bend." The shift from stanza to stanza shows a progression and, again, a total surrender to the declarative after line 24. The two instances of the perfect tense and one future verb refer to what is *thought*, all else being present tense.

Until the end of line 29, there have not been any verbs referring to sound except, distantly, "mourn" (line 27). But in the last four lines the words are "bleat," "sing," "whistles," and "twitter." It suggests that the deepening reverie has dimmed out the visual and all that remains is sound.

The eleven coordinate conjunctions aid the heaping up of impressions and nonurgency. Conjunctive adverbs of time collaborate in slowing down time, and a conjunctive adverb of cause "for" brings it to a standstill.

The numerous prepositional phrases suggest leisure and abundance. The six participial phrases refer to lushness and slow down the pace, although they also refer to progression—"conspiring . . . how to," then seeing to it, so to speak, and in the third stanza, the fait accompli.

The numerous infinitive phrases are dimmed out in the second and third stanzas, confirming the same effect of the participial phrases.

There are occasional inversions of word order in small segments: in "soft-lifted" there is gentleness; in "Think not" there is tiredness; and in "loud bleat" the accent is on loudness.

The grammatical elements and substructures of the poem suggest abundance, slow descriptiveness, a gathering and relinquishing, passiveness, growing reverie, surrender to invading impressions, and a dimming out of the visual, which gives way to sound. Keats has heaped up the images and slowed down time. The mood is passive, pleasant and distilled.

The rhetoric is unforceful. The addressee is the season of autumn, personified first as a solitary presence and then as nobody in particular. Presence is relinquished and the reverie takes over.

Tone and attitude are identical in this poem. There is no irony. It is an expression of relish for the beauties of autumn, mingling with reverie as in ancient pastoral fields, and increasing as the observer surrenders to it. We feel the tone quietly, as we would in a sunny field, taking off our coat and lying under a shady tree, closing our eyes and listening.

Words are particular and concrete, then general and widening out by turns. The effect is a deepening of the reverie.

The visual imagery *implies* color, but Keats withholds the name of any color until the words "rosy hue." The gradual shifts from visual to auditory begin to occur at line 22, and are fully achieved in the final stanza.

In the last three lines Keats triumphs in the art of pastoral poetry. The mood of languor, distilled by management of several structural aspects, reaches its acme. The imagery in the last stanza shows that following the question "Where are the songs of Spring?" a rich series of plural names of sounds that are "borne aloft," sinking, or heard from nearby ("crickets . . . soft treble") suddenly though quietly gives way to a singular noun, "redbreast." The single sound is a "whistle" heard from "a garden croft" somewhere, and then the ending widens out to a plural, a multitude ("gathering swallows"); the sound is distanced and confused (twittering) and lost "in the skies." The familiarity and simplicity of reference characteristic of Theocritus's pastorals is discovered to be deceiving as the almost unnoticed, unsparring management of the poet's art reveals its excellence.

Although I have discussed the grammatical and rhetorical elements, it is the *poetic* character, the structure of these elements, that has been effectual. Furthermore, the language, although simple, is figurative. The poem as a whole is a metaphor of which a literal expression might be "beauty is beguiling."

The poem has beauty and notable grace. It expresses inexhaustible abundance, which invades the senses so successfully that the drugged mind gradually relinquishes everything else; time stands still. This describes a progression from intent multiple awareness of visuality to a state of reverie in which the visual is abandoned. Awareness becomes single and auditory, and then widens out to the sounds from "the skies." The progress is quiet and easy, but something has shifted. A hidden force is expressed, somewhat like the gravity that draws a detached leaf from tree to earth on a still afternoon.

Keats prepares us for the moment of grace in the abundant first two stanzas. The actual moment of grace comes casually without exploiting itself in the deepening reverie. We feel the intuited counterforces retrospectively, although *counterforces* is too strong a word for what Keats delicately manages in lines 27 through 29. *Sustained excellence* describes it, rather, and in the second half of line 30, as if inevitably, without effort, the distillation of grace is completed.

Beauty

Whereas the sublime and the graceful both tend toward dynamic disequilibrium, the aesthetic quality of beauty expresses equilibrium. Disequilibrium is inequality between actual formal expression and the intuitive expectation of it in the receiver. If the sublime characterizes a meaning structure, the unexpressed potential seems to multiply, whereas the actual (the expression) seems to advance toward relative annihilation. Power accrues to the meaning. If grace qualifies the form, the actual expression exceeds expectation, and because the apparent ease of the expression takes the receiver by surprise, the receiver infers still unactualized potential, and power accrues to the agent or poet.

But in the *beautiful* structure, there is equality between the actual discovered interrelationships and the potential. The potential is perceived as qualitative and quantitative lures, which are hazards to unity. They are subtle and various and seem inexhaustible, but when unified relationship is discovered, the mind is drawn increasingly. The unactualized potential (suspicion of more to be discovered) accrues to the perfection of the structure itself.

Beauty is a prodigy of achievement of unity over variety, qualitative and quantitative. When in the aspects of complex material and formal elements we discover some native similarity, we perceive them as unified, and we experience pleasure. Variety is hazard that threatens unity, and the stimulated apprehension of relationship heightens awareness and affectivity. *Relevancies appear privileged and original.* Principality of some relevancies and subordination of others emerge, incarnating unity.

Not only are elements related, but relationships themselves are related by hazardous discoveries that make them seem inevitable. Proportion, in other words, is "due." Affectivity that accompanies discovery of proportion becomes impulsive enjoyment of relationship, creating the illusion that unity is inviolable and "organic." The unique mode of that particular and final relation that unifies all the relationships specifies the hierarchies in the posture of elements so that beauty is always experienced as a uniqueness.[56]

Beauty, that is, unity in variety, *equilibrium of relations despite almost prohibitive hazards*, is the central aesthetic quality in that it resides in the totality of the structure. The sublime, the tragic, and to some extent the comic, qualify mainly the meaning structure; grace resides mainly in the expression; but beauty is the success of the total organization of the elements. The literary work is a beautiful structure of substructures.

This does not mean that a beautiful work of art portrays only beautiful people and things. The totality of the organization of elements in the work is beautiful. The beauty of the person the work refers to (or in a painting, represents or pictures) would merit its own analysis, but the work as an organized whole is a triumph of unity over hazardous variety. Beauty is present.

Beauty in a particular feature or phase that engages our interest is frequently more recognizable than that which crowns a *gestalt*. Consequently, my observation in the above paragraph has been disputed from time to time. However, when we reflect on great tragedies, comedies, lyrics, or novels that refer to ugly people and objects, we do not therefore find the works lacking in beauty.

Another denial that beauty characterizes the object is exemplified by the popular dictum of Hume that beauty is "in the eye of the beholder."[57] Clearly, a perceptive beholder experiences the beautiful keenly, responding to the multiple hazards among related aspects of its elements, but the response is to the organization of an "object." This, too, is more convincing in the case of a painting, a statue, a person, a building, or a flower; a literary work is fashioned of words that are sounds with meanings, and sound and especially meaning are largely subjective, registered in the mind. Nevertheless, they are not totally subjective. The auditory nerve carries the impression of objectively caused verbal and musical sound to the brain, where it becomes an auditory image and, as such, becomes subjective. In language, the *imaged* sound conventionally refers to a specifically denoted object or meaning. The organization of such elements is an object too, although relationship depends for its actuality on the mind's perceiving relatabilities. In short, value, hence beauty, which is an aesthetic value, is to be characterized as both subjective and objective.

A homely clear proof can be recognized in that striking a "wrong" note or using a word that is a failure is offensive, and beauty is not.

It is true that what might be *considered* wrong by one person might not be considered so by another. There are such things as a "good ear" and "taste." Although taste can be cultivated, it is sometimes natural to a person. Moreover, a complex of ingredients experienced in a society during a given decade or half century conditions taste whether it be cultivated or natural. Thus, styles that appeal depend sometimes on things other than aesthetic merit. However, judgment free from prejudice seems to be fundamental to good taste. Taste, as such, good or bad, is expressed simply by what we *value*. Also, judgment, which decides in such cases, is an expression of knowledge, however such knowledge may have been obtained.

It is not uncommon now to hear critics and even aestheticians apologize for using the word *beauty*, the implication being that beauty is unimportant to modern advanced critics. Even those who have abandoned the word, and others who under many influences have repudiated the concept in their pursuit of shockingness, ugliness, violence, and so forth, affirm the quality by avoiding it.

Large segments of society still pursue beauty in one realm or another. By its nature it is guaranteed permanent appeal to humans, even were there not a vast deposit of genuinely beautiful literature pervading the civilizations of the world. The ideal is to know when shockingness, the ugly, the violent, are meaningful and clearly desirable in literature, and to understand them. But to enshrine irrelevance or chaos or any *element* of meaning exclusively is to err. It is safer to give an account of what one sees.

Although beauty could be exemplified in innumerable lyrics, I have chosen to use Shakespeare's Sonnet 73, a universal favorite.

That time of year thou mayst in me behold
When yellow leaves, or none, or few, do hang
Upon those boughs which shake against the cold,
Bare ruined choirs, where late the sweet birds sang.
In me thou seest the twilight of such day
As after sunset fadeth in the west,
Which by and by black night doth take away,

Death's second self that seals up all in rest.
In me thou seest the glowing of such fire
That on the ashes of his youth doth lie,
As the deathbed whereon it must expire
Consumed with that which it was nourished by.
　This thou perceiv'st, which makes thy love more strong,
　To love that well which thou must leave ere long.

Because the poem is made of artistically controlled language, its grammatical, rhetorical, and poetical aspects provide a good lens.

There are no unusual words; the vocabulary is unshowy and quiet, as if used without effort. Length of words contributes to the ease also; eighty-seven percent have one syllable, and the remaining thirteen percent have two. There are frequent archaisms—"thou seest," "perceiv'st," "doth," "fadeth," "his" to mean its, "thy," "ere." These tend to formalize and distance the language. Thus, effortless though the language is, it has a certain formality.

The sonnet shows deviant use of nonfigurative language—"late" for lately and "by and by" for gradually—making it tired, casual, suggestive of ripeness and authority. There is considerable circumlocution instead of directness—"That time . . . When . . . such fire . . . such day . . . That which it was nourished by . . . that . . . which thou must leave." This is denotative language veiled in relative clauses and appositional metaphors, as though it were reluctant and withholding, not releasing the meaning until the painful stab of the last five words.

The poem contains a notable number of abstract words—". . . time of year . . . day . . . west . . . Death . . . self . . . rest . . . youth . . . leave ere long."

Gradually it becomes clear that "time," which signals the opening of the poem, is its key. The realization dawns when we recognize the veiled twelfth line to be a compressed, universal, and masked reference to time. Quietly the pendulum alternation of "that," referring to time, then "this," summarily referring to the whole utterance to that point, and opens as on a hinge into the couplet and into that meaning himself. The grammar is effectual, seeming even by itself to serve the structure.

The speaker is addressing a loved person. He calls himself "me" regularly at the beginning of each quatrain, but after line 9 the word is replaced by the third-person "that" ("To love that well which thou must leave"). The shift makes the oncoming separation relentless, and reinforces the disciplined detachment that Shakespeare suggested in the realistic candor acknowledging old age and approaching death. We feel the effect in the release of the words "makes thy love more strong."

Shakespeare explicitly refers to the addressee three times after the disappearance of reference by the speaker to himself. The feeling is that the speaker is passive to receive love, again suggesting detachment. It is only retrospectively that his own love will come to mind, when the fact of the whole utterance becomes a proof. It occasions overtones in the reference to time, such as "late," "after sunset," and "by and by."

The last word "long" suggests a pun: the addressee will find it is too late; it accents the overtones in "take away" and "seals up." Also, the link between "must expire" and "must leave" is uncovered.

The rhetorical technique is thus a veiling circumlocution and understatement. There is a felt contrast between the muted detached address and the intensity of attachment, experienced retrospectively.

The sentences of each of the three quatrains, and the couplet, are complex, declarative, and loose. The effect of these similarities is that it makes the quatrains discrete and separate from each other and from the couplet. The declarative effects a mutedness of the (nevertheless) felt imperative. The loose structures, one following the other, give slowness and detachment to the meaning. Hinge words—"That time . . . When . . . such day . . . As . . . This . . ."—tie the whole together while keeping the quatrains discrete.

In the first and second quatrains, the last line is in apposition with a word in the third line; in the third quatrain, the third line, although not in apposition, has appositive meaning; and in the couplet, the last line is an appositive explanation of "love more strong."

Each quatrain has a basis of metaphor distinct from the others, reinforcing the discreteness of quatrains.

The vehicles of metaphor are uniformly rich throughout all three quatrains (autumn trees, twilight, ashes), but a delicate change appears in the tenors which begin with rich variety and gradually advance in the second and third quatrains toward reiteration; they move steadily into the compressed twelfth line, which quietly opens on an ironic universal perspective.

The effect is a vision of unity among several avenues of meaning. Consciousness stretches and there is exhilaration. Composure is regained in the words "This thou perceiv'st," which turn to a new shade and a fresh surge of meaning, namely that of the couplet. The *absence* of metaphor in the couplet, its brevity in relation to the quatrains, and the shift from the present tense of the quatrains into a future, tend to accent the tensions between "That time" (line 1) and the slipping away of it in the last two words (line 14).

Imagery is principally visual, advancing from particularized yellow to pervading red, then black, and then gray, suggesting passage to death. The only auditory image is an *echo* of sweet chirping no longer heard, reinforcing the tone of reluctance to lose what is precious, reluctance that deepens in the last line. Imagery vanishes entirely before the end of the last quatrain, underlining time's passing, and the couplet is empty of it.

The poet Coleridge considered onomatopeia to be the distinctly poetic character of poetry. This sonnet excels in it. The fitfulness of the pauses in line two suggests the capricious tug of the wind. "Those boughs" and "cold" have a large-mouthed hollow sound. "Shake against the cold" has guttural consonance suggesting creaking. "In "Bare ruined choirs" the quiet labial *b*, followed by a long vowel and a liquid *r*, is uncluttered, bare; ruined has a suggestion of a pun—rue—and the unstressed nasal following it comes like an echo in a corridor; the open echoing word "choirs" suggests opening into space, emptiness. In the second half line, "where late" prepares for a change and "the sweet birds sang" has sibilant chirping; the *ir* of "birds" has a robin's sound, and the nasal *ng* lingers. The second half line contrasts therefore with the emptiness and silence of the first. "Where late" shifts the line and a multitude of sweet sounds is thought of; "birds" is indiscriminate; what is explicit is "sweet." "Twilight" is a wide hushed sound. "Fadeth" shows decrease of sound in *th*, suggesting a fading. "By and by black night" is alliterated and the assonance has the regularity of a footstep. "Death's second self" has thumping assonance, punctuated by the end of the line, "seals up all in rest." The "second self . . . seals" alliteration echoes in the *s* of "rest." This supports the impression of the unquibbling silent approach of death. In the round uncluttered sound of "glowing" there is a surge of vitality. "Love that well which thou must leave ere long" has the character of a bell being struck, and the sound of "long" lingers for some time, clinging to its waning life.

The prosodic structure shows the last line of each of the first two quatrains as having seven stresses. This drops to six in the last line of the third quatrain, a crucial line; even the prepositional ending has only a secondary stress. But the last line of the couplet has *eight* stresses. So, looking to the last line of each quatrain and that of the couplet, one sees pattern in the number of emphasized syllables: seven, seven, six, eight. The last line of the poem takes on new prominence once this is noticed, and the emphasis reaches back into the ending of the preceding line— "love more strong." In the last line the word "love" occurs again: It is then seen in consonance with the word "leave," and these are the words that are felt to be in irremediable tension. There are other discoveries available to the prosodic consideration of the sonnet. The quietest line is the sixth, for instance. Also, there is new formality and stateliness in the recurrence of *l* and *th* in the couplet, and slow deliberateness in the word "which" dividing each of the last three lines into antithetic halves.

As is frequent in Shakespeare's sonnets, sound grows in importance in the final couplet, which is loud in the first half and quiet in the second. The word "long" slips away after being lightly said, following the abbreviated "ere"; but it then begins to echo and grow louder and louder, like a clear note from a tuning fork. The meaning vibrates like King Lear's "Never, never, never, never, never."

The central value is beauty. Being a sonnet, which is a species of lyric, it is static in reference. Thus, unlike the responses to dynamic reference of a plot that alternates between suspense and satisfaction, response to this sonnet is alternation between reflection and a seizing of ever wider realization, further reflection, and still wider realization. Whereas dynamic reference as such is linear, static reference is centrifugal.

We have seen that the poem is surprisingly structural in the grammatical and rhetorical aspects of the language used. The structural (poetic) aspects—samenesses and contrasts in kind, use and structure of sentences, and use of appositions—confirm the realization that the art (rational control of natural linguistic process) is directed to structure. It could hardly be denied that there is gradual discovery of order, or that the discovery is accompanied by surprise and expansion of awareness.

We have seen value where systems meet systems, and value emanating from the systems and from the purity of an aspect that these are related to. Not only is value occurrence the locus where system meets system, but the valuer is one of the elements. Aesthetic value is present when the valuer's desire, awakened by value, is simply the wish to continue to look at it, to contemplate it, to experience excitement as relatabilities are hazardously found (almost not found).

These particular features are notable in anything beautiful. Beauty is a prodigy of the success of unity over variety. When in aspects of elements or of substructures, some native similarity is discovered by a somewhat miraculous chance as if it were almost overlooked, a surprising unification is experienced with exhilaration. Beauty is necessarily subtle, thus hazardous, thus exciting, inviting us to continue looking.

The connotations form two main systems. "Yellow leaves" are associated with late splendor, hint of coming winter, reluctance. "Hang" is suggestive of limpness, enfeeblement, giving up, passiveness. "Boughs" connotes strength, stability, uplifting, striving. "Shake" suggests old age, ruthless wind, striving. "The cold" connotes bleakness, hostility. "Bare ruined choirs" reminds one of loneliness, gloom, loss, abandoned monasteries. "Sweet birds sang" contrasts with these, recalling past spring, summer, life. "Twilight" occasions a sense of quiet, ending, reminiscence, relinquishment. "Sunset" suggests redness, distance, splendor, ending. "Fadeth in the west" connotes almostness, forced relinquishment, awareness. "Black night" is nothingness, absoluteness, silence, sleep. "Death" as personified is relentless, nonregressive, mysterious. "Rest" is associated with ending, peace. "Fire" suggests impetuosity, destruction, heat. "Ashes" calls up grayness, dregs, uselessness.

These are reducible to systems, namely, meanings that refer to life, failure of life, and the tension between them. Life at its peak is felt in the purity of "sweet birds sang," and although failing, it clings to "day" and "glowing." Decline of life is connected with meanings of "none," "cold," "bare ruined," "black night," "Death's," "seals," "ashes," "deathbed." Reluctance to end hovers about the words "yellow leaves," "hang," "shake," "twilight," "sunset," and "fire . . . on the ashes."

The purity of vitality in "the sweet birds sang" is accented in the clauses's standing supreme in its system. It refers, however, to a remembered sweetness, no longer present. The preponderance of the connotations of failure of life gradually wins. Although its joyous lovely symbol stands prominent, echoing continuously, the power of its purity accents not life but the poignancy of its relentless passing. Cancelling out the effect of sweet birds approaches completeness in "black night" and "seals up," and in the forthright "must expire" and "must leave."

The valuer is one of the elements of the increasingly appearing value, reaching for still undiscovered relatabilities left by the poet's art. A closer look at "must" (line 11) finds the paradox "Consumed with that which it was nourished by" to be crucial. Time passes relentlessly, brings us to birth, to youth, to old age, and to death, just as fire nourishing wood turns it to ashes and is ultimately cooled by them.

Time quietly stands out as the central focus of meaning. The words "That time," "late," "after sunset," and "by and by," the masked line (12), and the almost soundless success of time in "must leave ere long" reinforce this observation. We realize the "choirs" have been buried by time's passing for centuries.

Shakespeare hints that the addressee sees only gradually, like the reader, in the progression, "thou mayest. . . behold," "thou seest," "This thou perceiv'st."

I find the conventional adherence to the art of the sonnet, in particular to the sonnet as developed by Shakespeare, is felt to be an added value, once the adventurousness of the stretch of meaning and the patterns of sound have exercised their own particular freedoms.

When the universality arising from such concreteness is further reflected upon and the fourteen-line limitation on the widening meaning is looked at; the harmony, the order in variety, that is, the beauty of the poem, continues to invite exploration.

Irony

Irony is sometimes merely a figure of speech. But tragic irony is a condition of a tragic plot; comic irony is a condition of a comic plot (or perhaps a momentary situation included in it). There is *dramatic irony* in, or independent of, dramatic literature. And there is also a philosophical or metaphysical irony attributed to many literary works as it is to events in real life.

In irony that is a figure of speech, the concept signified by words contrasts with concepts apprehended outside the frame created by the occurrence of the words. The purely ironic essence is always *in the focus upon the contrast.* An example would be naming a man who is "six feet four and large in proportion . . . Little Mildred," as Rudyard Kipling did in the short story "The Man Who Was."

Tragic ironies occur as interplay of parts of a whole structure. Macbeth, for instance, wanted to reign as king, free and unhampered. To do so he killed those in his way and thus hampered his freedom and position as king. *Tragic irony appears when the protagonist drives toward one thing in a sequence of actions that issues in what he is trying to avoid.* One set of conditions points toward one direction in an occurrence of *metaphysical* irony, and another set points toward the opposite.

In comic irony, as in dramatic irony as such, *a character says something intended to refer within a limited frame and the audience realizes the striking fitness of the remark to circumstances in a larger frame also, of which the speaker is unaware.* For instance, Chaunticleer says to Pertelote:

> Madame,
> Ye ben so scarlet reed aboute youre een,
> It maketh al my drede for to dyen;
> For al so siker as "*In principio*
> *Mulier est hominis confusio*"—
> Madame, the sentence of this Latyn is,
> 'Womman is mannes joye and al his blis'."[58]

The difference of perspectives of Chaunticleer and Pertolote can be seen, and the scope of these in turn, to be in contrast to the pilgrim listeners' and the reader's:

1. "Madame" befits a formal address to a dignified woman, but Pertelote is a barnyard hen.
2. Chaunticleer's balanced sentence structures mimic those of a rhetorical self-important hero, whereas he is an earthy male rooster.
3. Courtly love ladies were completely beautiful, but Pertelote is being flattered that she is red around the eyes, such redness being ugly and connoting drudgery.
4. Chaunticleer's forlorn hyperbole, that of a courtly lover, refers to the danger of dying in love, while Pertelote is pecking for seeds.
5. Chaunticleer quotes, like a learned scholar, the *In principio* opening of Saint John's gospel (and the beginning of Genesis!) referring to the eternity of the Godhead. But presently, he substitutes for the expected "was the Word, and the Word was with God" the mistranslation "woman is the confusion of man," the error betraying his less than honest and roosterly limitation.
6. Meanwhile, in Genesis, as the reader (like the smiling listeners on the pilgrimage) reflects, Eve was indeed the "confusio" of Adam.

7. Chaunticleer concludes in the amorous manner of a courtly
   lover, that when he feels her so soft by his side he would like
   to embrace her, but adds the practicality that their perch is too
   narrow.

In such characteristic juggling of ironies, frequent throughout
the *Canterbury Tales* and in the whirling speeches of Pandarus in
Troilus and Criseyde, irony spills plentifully beyond its target to
include another, or other targets. Thus, whereas the reader always has the upper hand, the joke is on one, both, or all of the
characters. In the above quotation from the *Nun's Priest's Tale*,
the reader (and the Canterbury pilgrims) enjoys the comic ex-
posure of both Chaunticleer and Pertelote in line 7, of Chaunticleer, in line 2, Pertelote in line 3, both Chaunticleer and
Pertelote in line 4, Chaunticleer in line 5, all men in line 6, and
Chaunticleer and Pertelote in line 7. Finally, the universality of
romantic love, in contrast to the unromantic interference by
commonplace inconvenience like that of the perch's limitation,
widens out the irony.

Bitter metaphysical irony, on the other hand, is habitually
exemplified in the poetry and novels of Thomas Hardy. For instance, in "A Wife in London,"[59] a young wife, while reading the
telegram announcing her husband's death "in the far South
Land" is handed a letter in "his hand, whom the worm now
knows." The letter is "page-full of his hoped return" and antici-
pates happiness and "new love that they would learn." The irony
lies in the simultaneity of the contrasting extremities of grief and
bliss.

In irony, richness is gained from contrast, in which there is
synthesis, since neither of the two or more areas is relinquished.
The operation peculiar to enjoyment or irony is synoptic, suspended between separation and synthesis. The contrasting elements are substructures of the artistic structure. A field of meaning occasioned by the particular positions of particular words,
no matter how remote its reach, can be part of the structure. The
effect of irony on the receiver is surprise at what is experienced
as sleight-of-hand compression of meaning.

Irony is located principally in the field of meaning, therefore,
even when it happens that words are ironic. In such an instance,
the denoted meaning of the words contrasts to another meaning
simultaneously realized.

Moreover, within the field of meaning, irony shows itself as a
contrast of far-reaching structures and substructures of the whole

structure. For instance, the impetuous drive of Oedipus to discover the culprit blinds him (though "seeing") to what the blind
(but seeing in another sense) prophet is saying to him; and his
ultimate self-inflicted blindness, concluding a still more impetuous drive, opens up his interior vision to "see" what he has
been.

The substructures are clusters of relationships: Some unrecog-
nized culprit has angered the gods by a crime against nature and
the gods have retaliated by killing off the citizens of Thebes in a
plague. Oedipus, informed of this and determined to find the
culprit, questions the blind prophet Tieresias and then rashly
ignores his warnings by issuing a decree of death or blindness in
exile to the still unknown culprit; the plague subsides. When,
through a chain of events gradually revealed, the actions of
Oedipus himself are found to have been the unknowing cause of
the curse on Thebes, he tears out his own eyes and goes into
exile. He is innocent in regard to the past actions that angered the
gods in that he acted in ignorance. The "blindness" of his own
impetuosity is balanced by the wisdom (vision) gained while he
endures his physical blindness. Pleas and complaints of the
chorus looking on widen the boundaries to include the whole
race of men and metaphysical realms seen as ironically related to
the incidents. The effect of these ironies is a bitter heightening of
the tragic meaning.

Comic meaning is hilariously enriched by irony, on the other
hand, not only in Chaucer's *Canterbury Tales* and *Troilus and
Criseyde*, books 1 and 3, but in the comedies of Ben Jonson, for
instance. Irony enriches or heightens meaning (tragic or comic),
and within the total meaning, *the ironic locus is in the tone*. In
literature tone is meaning that we experience as a result of *mutual understanding between the maker or speaker and the audience*. Both share a realization of the bitterness, or the fun, or
the sly amusement as the case may be. It is warranted by the way
the elements of the work are organized.

Because irony enriches meaning, it causes vibrations in the
audience; the wide fields of sublime and tragic meaning seem to
become wider. The audience continues to explore still wider
implications. It often happens that only later does the audience
feel the presence of the author. Because the "tone" is serious, the
speaker and the audience share for a considerable time the same
responses as the characters in the "plot." Gradually the audience
goes beyond them, seeing the work as an artistic whole.

The comic is radically different. Because comic characters are "less than we" in scale, and comic meaning is induced by shocking foreshortening, and because the audience has no affective response other than amusement at the plight of the characters, the tone is palpable, more likely to be noticed. Thus the *author* is applauded at once, and when the manipulations seem to be executed with ease, the art seems graceful. What must be noted, however, is that tone, like other areas of meaning, is part of the *structure*, and the suddenness of a shared glance between the author and the audience is an illusion created by the art. In Chaucer, tone is loud and clear, although he has been dead for almost six hundred years. The irony of satire is often "veiled," and response is gradual. Irony enriches and itensifies the effect. Sometimes, too, even satirical irony, while it is effective, can be gentle like that of Socrates. His speeches are presented in many of the dialogues of Plato, thus canonizing the phrase "Socratic irony."

Bitterness is heightened and frequently associated with irony in the modern short story such as Stephen Crane's *The Blue Hotel* or Hemingway's *The Killers*. The irony arises out of a well-managed dynamism of a plot.

In the latter story, for instance, Ole is hunted for having double-crossed someone, and Nick has just innocently double-crossed the killers. Irony is clear in the contrast between the efficiency of the distant Chicago machine and the paralysis in the lunchroom, between the aching awareness of some characters and the simple innocence of the others. There is exactness and purity in the planning of the story and power in the effect. The form itself is the end or purpose. Aesthetic value invites continuous contemplation. Retrospectively, the wider systems of value occurrence undergo increase and adjustment. Wider systems in *The Killers* include the Chicago machine and the still wider indiscriminate destructiveness of evil. It ends on a new horror, the possibility of the evil engulfing Nick.

The value is experienced as brute irony. Facts reported without comment assault the reader. Language with almost stupid clarity has the straight efficient aim of a gun. The art is disciplined.

Conclusion

BEFORE closing, I shall summarize the relation of aesthetic value to value as such. The aesthetic is one of several categories of value. It is distinguished from other kinds of value by the principle of its self-contained organization. An object of utilitarian value is radically related to systems outside of the valued object. An aesthetically valuable object is itself a system, of which all actual and potential relations are internal.

Thus, whereas a utilitarian value as such enables satisfaction of an external requirement (convenience, food, travel), an object characterized by aesthetic value fulfills the wish simply to look at or listen to or enjoy it by contemplating it. Unlike a useful thing or idea, which is fulfilled or completed in accord with its nature when someone who needs it uses it, the aesthetic object has internal coherence that is dynamically realized and fulfilled by being contemplated.

There are different modes of aesthetic structure. Although each crowns a unique work and exists as its peculiar excellence, aesthetic categories that have jelled in the course of history are guaranteed permanence by their endowment of the great literature of civilized nations.

The *sublime*, occasioned by language in the "grand style," characterizes the structure of meaning, and the reader experiences overwhelming power of increase. The *tragic*, occasioned by sometimes beautiful, but always serious, language, is centrally located in meaning that grows steadily to violence and destruction and arouses in the audience pity and terror. The *comic*, expressed in lower-than-average language (that of characters "below stairs" as distinct from that of kings and dukes they encounter), is shockingly actualized by foreshortened meaning of unexpectedly limited dimensions, making the audience laugh. *Grace* in literature, occasioned by unusual competence of language, characterizes meaning that occurs easily, flexibly, its reserves felt to be still unspent, and its excellence accruing to the author. *Beauty*, a nonutilitarian quality of a form, we experience as a hazardous union of elements that we gradually discover with increase of interest and adherence of the mind. *Irony*, expressed at any level of language, resides in *contrast* between chosen words and intended meaning, between immediate and remote meaning, or between the expected and the delivered meaning.

The reader who is weary of these theoretical abstractions might wonder where all of this leads. Generally, relief from weariness of an overdose is provided by the alternative, in this case something concrete. The theoretical comes to life only when it clarifies concrete experience of literature.

Meanwhile, clarity of thought regarding literary theory effects the clear presentation of it in classrooms, to be handed down to generations of students for the continued enrichment of civilized nations. One of the most central statements of this study is that *time is not an index of value*. Universities that are seasoned and independent are still teaching Homer, Sophocles, Virgil, Horace, Shakespeare, and Ben Jonson, as well as the best nineteenth- and twentieth-century authors, not because they are old or new but because they are supreme in their art.

Finally, in view of the deconstructionist effort, I might note that a genuine index of the value of a civilization is the intelligence and the depth of its appreciation of language and literature.

Notes

Introduction

1. Jacques Derrida, *Of Grammatology* (Baltimore: The Johns Hopkins University Press, 1976), lxxxix.

Chapter 1. Preliminary Distinctions: Rhetoric and Poetic

1. The art is explained by Charles S. Baldwin, *Ancient Rhetoric and Poetic* (Westport, Conn.: Greenwood Press, 1971). *See also* notes 4, 6, and 7.

2. The sharp Athenians were unconsciously in agreement with the Chinese philosopher Confucius, who is reputed to have said, "If everything were always called by its right name, all the ills of civilization would clear up."

3. *The Collected Dialogues of Plato*, ed. Edith Hamilton and Huntington Cairns. Bollingen Series 71: *Gorgias, trans.* W. D. Woodhead, 452E–453; *Phaedrus* 452E–453; *Phaedrus*, trans. R. Hackforth, 261D, 267D–273; Werner Jaeger, *Paideia* (New York: Oxford University Press, 1944), vol. 3, ch. 2.

4. Charles Sears Baldwin, *Medieval Rhetoric and Poetic* (Gloucester, Mass: Peter Smith, 1972); Henri-Irenée Marrou, *Saint Augustin et la fin de la culture antique* (Paris: E. de Boccard, 1938).

5. Aristotle, *The Basic Works of Aristotle*, ed. Richard McKeon (New York: Random House, 1941), 1355b26.

6. It is explained by Quintilian. *Institutio Oratoriae*, 3 vols. (Loeb Classical Library, 1921).

7. Aristotle, *Rhetoric* 1358a–b; cf. 1366a8–9.

8. It is radical departure because of the difference of ends, considered as purpose.

9. Craig La Drière, "Rhetoric and Poetic," in *Dictionary of World Literature*, ed. Joseph T. Shipley (Totowa, N.J.: Littlefield, Adams and Co., 1968), 342. The mixture of motives in rhetorically organized speech is successfully exposed by Terry Eagleton, *Literary Theory* (Oxford: Basil Blackwell, 1983), 148.

10. Eagleton, *Literary Theory*, 60, observes that "for phenomenological criticism, the language of a literary work is little more than an 'expression' of its inner meanings." Thus, there is "little place for language as such." For the classicist, on the other hand, the language is important material of which the structure is made. Eagleton agrees with the classicist position that meaning is dependent on language, and cites de Saussure (see n. 12).

11. Roman Jakobson says the language of literature is "organized violence committed on ordinary speech." See Eagleton, *Literary Theory*, 2.

12. See Ferdinand de Saussure, *Cours de linguistique générale* (Paris: Payot et Cie, 1922), 19, 25, 27–9; Aristotle *De Anima* 416b40, 427b21, 429b18, 430a10, 430a28ff., 431a4ff., 431–5; also Aristotle *Poetics* 1254a33.

13. Eagleton, *Literary Theory*, 127, says "Another way of putting Saussure's point about the differential nature of meanings is to say that meaning is always the result of a division of articulation of signs. The signifier 'boat' gives us the concept or signified 'boat' because it divides itself from 'moat'. The signified . . . is the product of the difference between two signifiers." It seems to me that de Saussure's "way of putting" it is clearer, because substituting *m* for *b* simply makes *boat* a different signifier from *moat*. By *product*, moreover, Singleton seems to mean *result*. His word *divides* probably means *distinguishes*.

14. The Old English word for *poet* was *scop*, the root of the perfect passive participle *(gescopen)* of the verb *sceapian*, "to shape." Also, the Greek word for *poet* (ποιητής) signified a maker, the word for *to make* being ποιεῖν.

15. A. C. Clark, *The Cursus in Medieval and Vulgar Latin* (Oxford University Press, 1910), 26, cites a confidential letter from Cicero to Atticus, using rhythmic patterns; cf. S. K. Brazzel, *The Clausulae in the Works of St. Gregory the Great* (Washington: The Catholic University of America Press, 1939), 23, who mentions rhythmic patterns in papal chancery documents; also S. R. Sullivan, *A Study of the Cursus in the Literary Works of St. Thomas More* (Washington: The Catholic University of America Press, 1943). The cursus rhythms were used in the Victorian era in Landor's "Pericles and Aspasia," *The Works of W. S. Landor*, ed. T. E. Welby (London: Chapman and Hall, 1927) X, 241–2.

16. William Cain, *The Crisis in Criticism* (Baltimore: The Johns Hopkins University Press, 1984), 248, regrets the instructing of bright graduate students of theory in Nietzsche, Marx, Derrida, and Foucault. Cain's comment is well directed since these men are not eminent for their contribution to the theory of literature.

17. The theory of anything includes cognition of its purpose, its origin or maker, the material it is made of, and its form (Aristotle *Physics* 2.7). The meaning of a literary work occasioned by the words and the way they are arranged (matter and form) may *refer* to history, politics, sociological and economic conditions, psychology, or religion. In a class of literary theory, reference made to any of these might be included as *reference*, an ingredient of the material.

Chapter 2. The Theory of Literature

1. Eagleton, *Literary Theory*, 2–3, 5.

2. Plato *Republic* 3. 38; also, 393C,395D1–3, 398A–B2, 607B1–C9.

3. Ibid., 607A4.

4. M. H. Abrams, *The Mirror and the Lamp* (New York: Oxford University Press, 1953), 7, 8–14, 30–46.

5. Donald Stauffer, *The Golden Nightingale* (New York: The Macmillan Company, 1949), 24–47.

6. Abrams, *Mirror and the Lamp*, 21–6, 70–155, 226–63.

7. See Amédée Ozenfant's essay, appendix to Etienne Gilson, *Painting and Reality* (New York: Pantheon Books, 1957), p. 4.

8. Yvor Winters, *The Anatomy of Nonsense* (Norfolk, Conn.: New Directions, 1942), passim.

9. See J. L. Sweeney, "Symbolism," in Shipley, *Dictionary*, 1968 ed., 409–10.

10. Susanne Langer, *Feeling and Form* (New York: Charles Scribner's Sons,

1953), 50; S. M. F. Slattery, "Looking Again at Susanne Langer's Expressionism," *British Journal of Aesthetics* (Summer 1987): 247–58.

11. See notes 2 and 3, chapter 2; cf. La Drière, "Classification," in Shipley, *Dictionary*, 1968, 63: "Modern distinctions between propaganda and literature of escape are of this kind."

12. La Drière, "Poetry and Prose," in Shipley, *Dictionary*, 1968 ed., 316.

13. Harold Osborne, *Aesthetics and Criticism* (New York: The Philosophical Library, 1955), 146, 148, 150, 152, 157, 169–70, 200; also Wing-tsit-Chan, "Expressionism," in *Enclycopedia of the Arts*, ed. Dagobert Runes and Harry Schrickel (New York: Philosophical Library, 1946), 340.

14. La Drière, "Organic Form," in Shipley, *Dictionary*, 1968 ed. 71, quoting Coleridge, *Lectures on Shakespeare*, 1, *Coleridge's Shakesperean Criticism*, ed. Thomas M. Raysor (Harvard College, 1958), Lecture 1.

15. See David Daiches, "Imagism," in Shipley, *Dictionary*, 1968, ed. 221; also Slattery, "What Is Literary Realism?" *Journal of Aesthetics and Art Criticism* 21 (Fall 1972): 55–62.

16. Anna Elizabeth Balakian, *Literary Origins of Surrealism* (New York: King's Crown Press, 1947), 79.

17. Michel Carrouges, *André Béton et les données fondamentales du surréalisme*, sixième édition (Paris nrf. Gallimard, 1950), 15, 35, 74, 93–95, 103.

18. Ibid., 16.

19. Ibid., 17, 35, 74.

20. Ibid., 75, 76, 118.

21. Ibid., 74, 108.

22. Balakian, *Literary origins*, 2; also Osborne, *Aesthetics and Criticism*, 202.

23. Sidney Zink, "Poetry," in Runes and Schrickel, *An Encyclopedia;* Cain, in the preface to *Crisis in Criticism*, xi, writes, "I have often found myself growing impatient with theory . . . since theory has come close to exhausting itself." Accurate theory does not exhaust itself; inaccurate theory and the energy of inaccurate theorists are probably the cause of his impatience. William Ray, *Literary Meaning* (Oxfordshire: Basil Blackwell, 1984), 142, notes intelligently "the necesity of keeping theory and practice within sight of each other."

24. See Roman Ingarden, *The Literary Work of Art* (Evanston, Ill.: Northwestern University Press, 1973), 10, 29, 56–63 esp.

25. This actualization is unique and subtle, an occurrence that, although frail, is real, actualized. However, see Gayatri Chakravorty Spivak's preface to Derrida, *Of Grammatology*, lxxxix. Of course, even a person's two readings of a book can be different, depending upon the mind's experiences in the interim between them.

26. However, Joseph Strelka, in his foreword to *Problems of Literary Evaluation* (University Park, Pennsylvania: Pennsylvania State University Press, 1969), viii, understandably regrets "these times of uncertainty about values" and complaints of "some people" about "the uncertainty of values at all times." In 1973, Roman Ingarden, *Literary Work of Art*, 7, said, "At this point we do not know what distinguishes a work that has value from a work that is worthless, nor . . . what it means when a work has value . . . in particular, *literary* value."

27. Plato Ion 553D^N, 535A, 536A—C.

28. Carrouges, *André Breton*, 17, 35, 74.

29. See "Milieu," in Shipley, *Dictionary*, 1968 ed., 272; also Balakian, *Literary Origins*, 2, and Carrouges, *André Bréton*, 9–10, 108–11.

30. Winters, *Anatomy of Nonsense*, passim.

31. Aristotle *Poetics* 1447a29.

32. Walter Jackson Bate, ed., *Criticism: The Major Texts* (New York: Harcourt Brace Jovanovich, 1970), Intro. 3.

33. Artistotle *Poetics* 1451b1–5, b28–9, 1457a18–24.

34. Alexander Pope, "Preface to Shakespeare," in *The Works of Shakespeare* (Oxford: Printed at the Theater, 1744), 1, x; John Dryden, "Original and Progress of Satire," in *Essays of John Dryden*, ed. W. P. Ker (Oxford: Clarendon Press, 1900), 92; Samuel Johnson, "Pope," in *The Complete Works of Samuel Johnson*, ed. Arthur Murphy (London: J. Nichols and Son, 1810), 2, 193, 169, 268.

35. Plato *Ion* 533D1–534D4.

36. La Drière, "Scientific Method," in Shipley, *Dictionary*, 1972 ed., 365.

37. To say it is simply that does not explain the "extraordinary" natural propensity. It is subtle. See Bernard Lonegan, *Insight* (New York: The Philosophical Library, 1970), esp. 4, 418–19, 704.

38. The "proof" has been enlisted as the indication from the beginning. The word *genius* is very old. The *pater familias*, or priest of the household in Roman families of the fifth century B.C., was said to have an indwelling spirit called a *genius*.

39. Plato *Phaedrus* 245A; also Dominique Bouhours, *Les Entretiens d'Ariste et d'Eugène* (Paris: Gabriel Huart, 1691), 317.

40. Pope, *The Iliad of Homer Translated by Mr. Pope* (London: Printed by W. Bowyer for Bernard Lintott, 1715) notes to bk. 13, line 15, and bk. 15, l. 86.

41. *Ibid.*, bk. 15, note to l. 20; *also*, "Essay on Homer's Battles," *Iliad*, vol. 2, pp. 322–26; "Preface to the *Iliad* (Oxford: Shakespeare Head Press, 1936), p. 94; Letter to Cromwell, 12 November 1711, Elwin-Courthope ed. of Pope's *Works*, vol. 6, p. 127.

42. Robert Kilburn Root, *The Poetical Career of Alexander Pope* (Princeton: Princeton University Press, 1941), 27. The word *wit* is a burdened word.

43. Slattery, *The Pursuit of Grace in the Technique of the Poetic Process according to Alexander Pope*, Microcard Ph.D. diss. (Washington, D.C.: The Catholic University of America Press, 1952), 99.

44. J. E. Sandys, *A History of Classical Scholarship* (Cambridge: Cambridge University Press, 1921), 1, chap. 1.

45. T. S. Eliot, "Tradition and the Individual Talent," in *Selected Essays* (New York: Harcourt Brace, 1950). 5.

46. Henry James, "Preface to *The Spoils of Poynton*," in *The Art of the Novel*, ed. R. P. Blackmur (New York: Charles Scribner's Sons, 1953), 119. See also "Preface to *The Portrait of a Lady*," in Blackmur, *Art of the Novel*, 43.

47. *Ibid.*

48. James, "Preface to *The American*, in Blackmur, *Art of the Novel*, 23.

49. James, "Preface to *The Portrait of a Lady*," in Blackmur, *Art of the Novel*, 44.

50. James, "Preface to *The Aspern Papers*," in Blackmur, *Art of the Novel*, 163.

51. James, "Preface to *The Lesson of the Master*," in Blackmur, *Art of the Novel*, 230.

52. H. Granville-Barker, *Prefaces to Shakespeare* (Princeton: Princeton University Press, 1963), 174–213.

53. George Beiswanger, "Doing and Viewing Dances," *Dance Perspectives* 55 (Autumn 1973): 8–13.

54. Edward Bullough, " 'Psychical Distance' as a Factor in Art and an Aesthetic Principle," in *Aesthetic Lectures and Essays by Edward Bullough*, ed. Elizabeth Wilkinson (Stanford, Calif.: Stanford University Press, 1957), 114.

55. Brewster Ghiselin, "The Light and the Crystal," *Sewanee Review* 67 (1959): 131–35.

56. Pope, "Essay on Criticism," 1. 174.

57. Ibid., 82–87, 163–64.

58. For this prosodic notation see La Drière, "Prosody," in Shipley, *Dictionary*, 1968 ed., 325.

59. Murphy, ed., *The Complete Works*. See *Idler* 60 (7:238); *Rambler* 101 (5:194); *Rasselas* 3 (pp. 53, 330–31, 338); *Idler* 3 (7:10); "Young" (vol. 11:286–346).

60. Melvin Rader, "The Outsider," *Journal of Aesthetics and Art Criticism* 16 (March 1958): 313.

61. Cicero *Orator*, (Loeb Classical Library, 1939), 70–74.

62. Edward Young, "Conjectures on Original Composition in 1759," in *Critical Theory since Plato*, ed. Hazard Adams (New York: Harcourt Brace Jovanovich, 1971), 338–47.

63. Horace *The Art of Poetry*, ed. and trans. Walter Jackson Bate, in *Criticism: The Major Texts* (New York: Harcourt Brace Jovanovich, 1970), 56–7.

64. William Wordsworth, "Preface to the Second Edition of Lyrical Ballads," in Bate, *Criticism*, 432–3.

65. T. S. Eliot, "Tradition," 29.

66. Pope, "Essay on Criticism," 88–90, 136–40, 141–64. Jean-Francois Lyotard, *The Postmodern Condition* (Minneapolis: University of Minnesota Press, 1979), 81, writes, "The post-modern . . . artist and the writer . . . are working without rules in order to formulate the rules of what *will have been done*." This describes working by trial and error. The chances are that if this is so, the future will be less productive than the past. However, at every turn they seem to me to be using rules. And if they are working in order to formulate rules, they are not wise. All that Lyotard means, I suspect, is that they are experimenting like men of the past.

67. Ibid., 660.

68. *Minos* (Loeb Classical Library, 1927), 316D—E.

69. Pope, "Essay on Criticism," 147.

70. Ibid., 88–89.

71. Ibid., 149.

72. Slattery, "Henry James' Theory of Literary Invention," *The Greyfriar Lectures*, Second Series (Loudonville, N.Y., 1959), 18, 19.

73. Murphy, *The Complete Works*, 3:338.

74. Slattery, *Hazard, Form and Value* (Detroit, Mich.: Wayne State University Press, 1971), 62–63.

75. Sigmund Freud, "Creative Writers and Daydreaming," in Adams, *Critical Theory*, 749–53.

76. Abrams, *Mirror and the Lamp*, chaps. 4, 5, 6, 9.

77. David Hume, *A Treatise of Human Nature* (New York: E. P. Dutton and Company, 1939), 13, 17–19, 20–21; Celestine Bittle, *Reality and the Mind* (New York: Bruce Publishing Company, 1936), 317.

78. Words of poetry were traditionally described by poets of the past as "golden."

79. Language belongs to humans alone on the earth. By it, we communicate with other beings of our own kind, relating our experiences and learning those

of others. By writing we can extend our communicating beyond the limits of time and space. It enables us to organize our thinking, to reason, and to create. The primitive roots of language as it originated on the earth, and developed, are thought to have been 39 in number, and through the course of human history 138 have formed, not counting the numerous dialect formations in tribal communities. See W. L. Chafe, "Language," in *The New Catholic Encyclopedia*, 8 (New York: McGraw-Hill, 1967), 367–73.

80. See LaDrière, "Form," in Shipley, *Dictionary*, 1968 ed., 167–71.

81. The language of poetry differed from that of prose for centuries. The difference stems from the purpose for which each was used. Aristotle said no one uses "fine language for teaching geometry."

82. La Drière, "Voice and Address," in Shipley, *Dictionary*, 1968 ed., pp. 441–44.

83. Here again, a difference between the terminologies of Ingarden's *Literary Work of Art* and this study is noticeable. Ingarden's "phonic form" is here called *sound structure*, his "concretized" is here rendered as *actualized*; his "real" is here *denoted*; and his words for sounds, "timeless, unchangeable entities," are here designated as *actual denotative occurrences*.

84. De Saussure, *Cours de linguistique générale*, 28.

85. Lyotard, *The Postmodern Condition*, 3–4, 81, understandably claims phonology, linguistics, cybernetics, modern algebra and informatics, computer "languages", telematics, intelligent terminals, and paradoxology to be language. It is important to note that this is metaphorical use of the term *language*. He briskly adds, "The nature of knowledge cannot survive unchanged within this context of information. . . . We may expect . . . exteriorization of knowledge with respect to the 'knower'." This is doubtful. The *nature* of knowledge will survive unchanged; it is the *extent* of it that will increase. The nature of the brain will not increase, in all probability.

86. William Wordsworth, "Preface to the Second Edition of Lyrical Ballads," 433ff; Coleridge, *Biographia Literaria*, ch. 14, *Crit. Theory since Plato*, ed. Hazard Adams, p. 471.

87. Rhyme, regularity of rhythm and unprosaic language appear in Wordsworth's "Ode: Intimations of Immortality," "Ode to Duty," "The Solitary Reaper," "Elegiac Stanzas," the ten sonnets, and "Extempore Effusion upon the Death of James Hogg." Moreover, although *The Prelude* is blank verse, the language is not everywhere that of plain prose.

88. La Drière, "Comparative Method in the Study of Prosody," in *Comparative Literature, Proceedings of the ICLA Congress*, ed. W. P. Friedrich (Chapel Hill: University of North Carolina Press, 1949), 10.

89. Slattery, *Hazard, Form and Value*, 28.

90. This is *potency*, the alternative to actuality. The importance of the reality at the heart of this Aristotelian dichotomy is underestimated.

91. "Form or essence . . . is the end of the process of becoming" (Aristotle *Metaphysics* 1015a10; cf. 1917b22–25, 1018b8–10, 1032a12). In literature, aspects of form are perceivable as mutuality of reference, as connection between the question that creates suspense and the answer that resolves it, between character and character, between sound and sound (alliteration, rhyme, etc.), between metaphorical vehicle and tenor. In the deconstructionist view is seen only *continuance* of becoming.

92. William Shakespeare, *As You Like It* 2.1.2.

93. Cf. the published paper of Craig La Drière's lecture edited by Böckmann in *Stil- und Formprobleme in der Literatur* (Heidelberg: C. Winter, 1959), 34.

94. René Wellek and Austin Warren, *The Theory of Literature* (New York: Harcourt Brace Jovanovich, 1956), 157.

95. T. S. Eliot, "Tradition," 7.

96. Paul Schrecker, *Work and History* (Princeton: Princeton University Press, 1948), 59.

97. St. Thomas Aquinas, *Summa Theologica*, trans. Fathers of the Dominican Province (New York: Benziger Bros., 1947), 1, 45, 2; 1, 41, 5; 1, 50, 2; 1, 44, 4, *Obj.* 3; 1, 54, 3, *Reply Obj.* 2; 1, 58, 2; also his *Commentary on Aristotle's De Anima*, trans. Kenelm Foster and Silvester Humphries (London: Routledge and Kegan Paul, 1851), Bk. 2, *Lectio* 1, 216; *Lec.* 5, 281; *Lec.* 6, 304 and 315.

98. John Laird, *The Idea of Value* (Cambridge: Cambridge University Press, 1929), 36. Joseph Strelka, "Foreword," *Problems of Literary Evaluation* mentions concerning "these times" that they are characterized by "uncertainty about values."

99. Clearly the viewpoint of this study is opposed to that of Northrop Frye as quoted in Joseph Strelka's *"Problems of Literary Evaluation,"* 17. It seems to me that general knowledge about value is not only desirable but indispensable.

100. Slattery, *Hazard, Form and Value*, 79–89, 90, 92–97.

Chapter 3. Value

1. Money has value in exchange whereas the other items have value in use. The difference, however, is immaterial to the point being made here.

2. Aquinas, *Commentary* 2.11.266; also, Slattery, *Hazard, Form and Value*, 64–66.

3. Jonathan Culler, *On Deconstruction*, Ithaca, N.Y.: Cornell Univ. Press, 1982, 86, says well, "Causality is . . . basic. . . . We could not live or think as we do without taking for granted that one event causes another, that causes produce effects. The principle of causality asserts the logical and temporal priority of cause and effect." This has not been universally held, however. Hume, *Treatise of Human Nature*, denied not only reality to any substance (1, 1, 6) or persons (1, 4, 35), but also to causality (1, 3, 14*ff.*).

4. On the other hand, Culler, *On Deconstruction*, 226, says deconstruction emerges from the writings of Derrida and de Man only by dint of iteration, citation, deviation, distortion, and parody.

5. Aquinas, *Summa Theologica* 1.45.1, Reply Obj. 2; 1.47.3; 1.44.4, Obj. 3.

6. Northrop Frye, "Contexts of Literary Evaluation," *Problems of Literary Evaluation*, ed. Joseph Strelka (n. 26, chap. 2), pp. 14–21, says "The sense of value is an individual, unpredictable, incommunicable, indemonstrable, and mainly intuitive reaction to knowledge." I am, by implication, deleting "unpredictable," "incommunicable," and "indemonstrable."

7. Although it is not written anywhere, La Drière said in class, "Meaning is relation; value is relation apprehended as requiredness" (see also chap. 3, n. 2).

8. Eric Donald Hirsch, Jr., "Privileged Criteria in Literary Evaluation," in Strelka, *Problems*, 22–23, says, "Aristotle was wrong to suppose that human productions can be classified in a definitive way." I do not agree.

Chapter 4. Aesthetic Value and Affective Hazard

1. Slattery, *Hazard, Form and Value*, 93–97, 71–73. Eagleton, *Literary Theory*, says "value" is "a transitive term. . . . Shakespeare would be no more valuable than much present-day graffiti" in another culture and time. And

"though many people would consider such a social condition tragically im-
poverished, it seems to me dogmatic not to entertain the possibility that it might
arise rather from a general human enrichment."

However, value is a result of a cluster of conditions. Eagleton means, I
suspect, that there has to be a valuer. True, but in the valued object or situation
there are objective features (if not, why "impoverishment" for "many" people?).
Eagleton continues (p. 12–13), "I do not mean that it is unstable because value
judgments are subjective. . . . Facts are public and . . . unimpeachable, values
are private and gratuitous." Eagleton's writing is engaging and unquibbling,
with frequent exemplification. But I maintain that the conditions of value are in
the structure of the object. Value is "subjective" in so far as it takes recognition
of these conditions to *actualize* it.

2. Wellek, *Theory of Literature*, ix, said, "The work of art . . . is itself a
structure of values." It was a genuine insight. Roman Ingarden, *The Cognition of
the Literary Work* (Evanston, Il.: Northwestern University, 1973) sees the literary work as an aesthetic "object," a conviction he repeats in *Selected Papers in
Aesthetics* (Washington D.C.: The Catholic University of America Press, 1985),
11, n. 10 of "general assertions."

3. George Boas's amusing essay, ("The Problem of Literary Evaluation," in
Strelka, ed. *The Yearbook of Comparative Criticism*, Vol. 2, p. 9*ff*.) shows
insights concerning nonliterary "values." He ends his discussion wanting aesthetic values too, but he stops short of probing them. However, his remark (p. 9)
"There is no value in the absence of human beings who do the valuing" is true,
and thus not to be lost. There must be potential value in the object, of course.

4. The Russian Formalists, although influenced by phenomenology, were
saved from the totally Neoplatonist enlargement of focus by their term
bracketed off. It is not as descriptive of the literary work as Aristotle's "beginning, middle and end," since in bracketing off, the middle might not develop as
such from the beginning, nor the end from the middle.

5. Wlad Godzich, "The Deconstruction of Derrida" in *The Language of
Criticism and the Sciences of Man* [proceedings of the 1966 Symposium at
Johns Hopkins University 1970], 11), says that deconstructionist Paul de Man,
who was "trained in close reading at Harvard . . . in philosophical inquiry in
Europe, began to explore the possibility of a critical practice based upon its
most fundamental act: reading." This seems to me, as I suspect it does to
Godzich, to have been misguided. The fundamental act of "critical practice" is
evaluation, and this is based on knowledge of value. Reading is the beginning
only.

6. Georg Wilhelm Hegel, *Phänomenologie des Geistes* (Frankfurt am Main:
Suhrkamped, 1970), 35, seems to have been thinking of this matter when he
observed that what is familiarly known is not properly known. On the other
hand, displaying an idea in its original elements means "returning upon its
moments" (see Spivak's preface to Derrida, *Of Grammatology*, xiii). The idea
expressed by Hegel is that knowing is hindered by familiarity, whereas the
point I am making is that *interest* or *excitement*, not knowledge, is reduced by
familiarity (unhazardousness). Spivak adds (ibid., xiii) that Rousseau was "mel-
ancholy" about what he called the "broken immediateness" of the "experience
of too pronounced a familiarity." However, it is simply that attention wanders in
response to too pronounced a familiarity. It is the reader or observer who
changes; the observed reality need not.

7. Slattery, *Hazard, Form and Value*, 11–12.

8. Aristotle *Poetics* 1451b5*ff*.

9. Slattery, *Hazard, Form and Value*, 73.

10. Leonard B. Meyer, "Meaning in Music and Information Theory," *Journal of Aesthetics and Art Criticism* 15 (June 1957), 412–24.

11. Samuel Taylor Coleridge, "Shakespeare, A Poet Generally," in *Coleridge's Lectures on Shakespeare* ed. Ernest Rhys (New York: E. P. Dutton, 1907), 46ff.

12. Slattery, *Hazard, Form and Value*, 62–63.

13. See chapter 3, note 2.

14. Slattery, *The Pursuit of Grace*, 192–97.

15. David S. Miall, "Aesthetic Unity and the Role of the Brain," *Journal of Aesthetics and Art Criticism* vol. 35 (1976), 57–67.

16. In plainer terms, aesthetic values (beauty, grace, sublimity, irony, comicness), in their individual ways draw attention to the object, beguiling the reader to acceptance of the whole with whatever values it expresses. Horace *Ars Poetica*, lines 99–100 observes that "poems should be not only beautiful but graceful too, thus drawing us wherever they will."

Chapter 5. Aesthetic Values in Literature

1. Northrop Frye, "Contexts," 21, says, "Values cannot be demonstrated." It seems to me that they have to be.

2. Longinus, *On the Sublime*, 2d ed., ed. and trans. William Rhys Roberts (Cambridge: at the University Press, 1907). Available also in Adams, *Critical Theory*, 77–102, and in Bate, *Criticism: The Major Texts*, 62–75.

3. Immanuel Kant, *Critique of Judgment*, in Adams, *Critical Theory*, 2, 23, 24, 26, 27–28, 391–96. Samuel Johnson, *Rambler*, 94, 9 Feb. 1751. Joseph Addison *Spectator* 412, 23 June 1712. Pope, *Notes to Iliad* Book 2, line 950; Bk. 5, l. 116; Bk. 8, l. 370; Bk. 15, l. 396; Bk. 21, l. 290. *The Iliad of Homer Translated by Mr. Pope* (London: W. Bowyer for Bernard Lintot, 1715). John Dennis, "The Advancement and Reformation of Modern Poetry,", 4–6, in Adams, *Critical Theory*, 273–76.

4. Aquinas, *Summa Contra Gentiles*, ed. in *Basic Writings of Saint Thomas Aquinas*, ed. Anton Pegis (New York: Random House, 1944), 1.3. He refers to the idea of Aristotle, *Nicomachean Ethics* 1.3, 1094b24; cf. Aristotle *De Caelo et Mundo* ibid. 291b26.

5. Carrouges, André Bréton, 75, 76, 118. Also Elliot Grant, ed., *French Poetry of the Nineteenth Century* (New York: Heath and Co., 1956), 364.

6. Raymond Bayer, *L'esthétique de la grâce*, vol. 2 (Paris: Librairie Felix Alcan, 1933), 332.

7. Samuel Holt Monk, "A Grace beyond the Reach of Art," *The Journal of the History of Ideas* 5 (1944): 131–50; Raymond Bayer, *L'esthétique de la grâce*, Intro.

8. See Slattery, *The Pursuit of Grace*, 290. note 380.

9. Teodor Dostoevsky, *The Idiot* (New York: Dutton, 1934), 4, 5.

10. Aristotle *Poetics* 1453a10–30.

11. Longinus, *On the Sublime*, 9.

12. Aristotle *Physics* 236b20–237a12. For the phenomenologist "time is . . . the very structure of human life, something I am made out of . . . the inner dynamic of my constant transcendence" (Eagleton, *Literary Theory*, quoting Heidegger who "seeks to return to pre-Socratic thought"). Aristotle's idea seems more accurate, that time is the "measure of motion in respect of before and after."

13. *Beowulf, ed.* Friedrich Klaeber, third edition (Boston: Heath, 1950), line 1:
"Hwaet we Gardena in geardagum . . ."
(Lo, we the Spear-Danes in days of old . . .)
14. "Preface to the *Iliad,*" See ch. 2, note 41.
15. *Beowulf,* line 455. Usually the words *se Wealdend* (ruler), *se Helm* (protector) or *God* (God) were used, but *se Wyrd* (Necessity, Destiny) was invoked by Beowulf in a speech to Hrothgar the king before the encounter with Grendel.
16. Aristotle *Poetics* 1448a4.
17. *The Iliad of Homer, Translated by Mr. Pope* (London: W. Bowyer for Bernard Lintot, 1715), notes to Bk. 8, line 363; Bk. 2, line 572; Bk. 1, line 694; Bk. 20, line 1137. See also Ault, *Preface to the Iliad,* 224–25.
18. Horace *Ars Poetica* 40–41, 217; 309–11; *Epistle* 2, 1; "Epistle to Augustus," 390–95; *Satires and Epistles,* ed. J. B. Greenough (Boston: Ginn and Co., 1890).
19. *Preface to the Iliad* [in Ault's] *The Prose Works of Alexander Pope;* also, in old Lib. of Congress books Pope, tr. *The Iliad of Homer* notes 1, 229, 572, 683, and "Postscript," *The Odyssey of Homer.*
20. In the sublime as diagrammed earlier, the hidden force is felt to be in the too-much-to-manage meaning to be expressed; in the graceful, the force appears to be in the capacity of the agent who manages the meaning with ease.
21. Pope, *The Iliad of Homer* note to Bk. 2, line 950.
22. "Preface . . . *Iliad,*" Ault ed., 1, 235.
23. Slattery, *The Pursuit of Grace,* 290.
24. Pope, "Essay on Crit.," edd. Elwin and Courthope (London: John Murray, 1871), Vol. 2, pp. 33*ff.,* line 365.
25. Plato *Ion* 535B6, C7.
26. Alfred Lord, *Singer of Tales* (Cambridge: Harvard University Press, 1960), passim.
27. Lord said this in an unpublished lecture at New York University.
28. Lord, *Singer of Tales,* 151, 129, 133, 149, 152.
29. See *Beowulf,* line 88.
30. Aristotle *Poetics* 1451a24–30.
31. Ibid., 1453a17.
32. Bullough, *Aesthetic Lectures,* 112.
33. Aristotle *Poetics* 1452b1–2; 32 1453b1.
34. Ibid., 1449b25.
35. Ibid., 1449b27.
36. Shakespeare (1564–1616) knew Latin. There were Latin translations of the *Poetics* (Vahlen, 1519; Valgrisi, 1550; Vittori, 1573). Cf. H. Palmer, *List of English Editions, Translations of Greek and Latin Classics before 1641* (London: Blades, East and Blades, 1911), 15ff.
37. Aristotle *Poetics* 1449a32.
38. See pp. 71–72, 73, 74, 75–77, and 98–99 for classically comic features.
39. Demetrius, *On Style,* trans. William Rhys Roberts (Cambridge: The University Press, 1902), 133, 140.
40. La Drière, *Stil-und Formprobleme in der Literatur,* ed. P. Böckmann (Heidelberg: C. Winter, 1959), 34–36.
41. Slattery, *The Pursuit of Grace,* 15–32.
42. Ibid., 60–68.

43. Dominique Bouhours, *Les Entretiens*, passim.

44. Bayer, *L'esthétique de la grâce*, vol. 1, 20, 73, 90–91, 291, 292, 357.

45. Ibid.

46. Horace *Ars Poetica* lines 99–100.

47. Slattery, *The Pursuit of Grace*, 15–69.

48. Ibid., 248.

49. The *Odyssey* Bk. 5, l. 338; Bk. 6, lines 18 and 223–245; Bk. 7, l. 5; Bk. 8, l. 364; Bk. 14, l. 267.

50. Plato *Phaedrus* 227D; 234–235a; cf. Aristotle *Nicomachean Ethics* 1127b23–32; b34–1128b9.

51. Homer, *Iliad*, Pope's note 5, 517; Plato *Phaedrus* 227D, 234b–235A.

52. Slattery, *The Pursuit of Grace*, 32–40.

53. Ibid., 43–46.

54. Philippe-Ernst Le Grand, *Etude sur Théocrite* (Paris: Ancienne Librarie Thorin et Fils, 1898), 103, 140, 150, 170–72.

55. Ibid., 413–29.

56. Slattery, "Beauty in Aesthetics," *The New Catholic Encyclopedia* (New York: McGraw Hill, 1967), 2, 207–8.

57. David Hume, "Of the Standard of Taste," in Adams, *Critical Theory*, 315.

58. Geoffrey Chaucer, "The Nun's Priest's Tale," lines 4350–4356, in *The Works of Geoffrey Chaucer*, 2d ed., ed. F. N. Robinson (Boston: Houghton Mifflin Company, 1961), 203.

59. *The Complete Poems of Thomas Hardy*, ed. James Gibson (New York: Macmillan Publishing Company, 1976), 91–92.

Bibliography

Abrams, M. H. *The Mirror and the Lamp.* New York: Oxford University Press, 1953.

――――. "Preface." In *The Norton Anthology of English Literature.* New York: W. W. Norton, 1968.

Adams, Hazard, ed. *Critical Theory Since Pato.* New York: Harcourt Brace Jovanovich Inc., 1971.

Addison, Joseph. *The Spectator.* Cincinnati: Applegate and Company, 1862.

Aquinas, Saint Thomas. *Commentary on Aristotle's De Anima.* Translated by Kenelm Foster and Silvester Humphries. London: Routledge and Kegan Paul Limited, 1951.

――――. *Summa Contra Gentiles.* In *Basic Writings of Saint Thomas Aquinas,* edited by Anton Pegis, 3–224. New York: Random House, 1944.

――――. *Summa Theologica.* Translated by Fathers of the Dominican Province. New York: Benziger Brothers, Incorporated, 1947.

Aristotle. *De Anima.* Translated by J. A. Smith In *The Basic Works of Aristotle,* edited by Richard McKeon, 535–603. New York: Random House, 1941.

――――. *On the Heavens.* In McKeon, *The Basic Works.* Translated by J. L. Stocks, 396–466.

――――. *Metaphysics.* In McKeon, *The Basic Works.* Translated by W. D. Ross, 681–926.

――――. *Nicomachean Ethics.* In McKeon, *The Basic Works.* Translated by Ross, 935–1112.

――――. *On the Art of Poetry.* In McKeon, *The Basic Works.* Translated by Ingram Bywater, 1455–87.

――――. *Physics.* In McKeon, Ibid. *The Basic Works.* Translated by R. P. Hardie and R. K. Gaye, 218–394.

――――. *Rhetoric.* In McKeon, *The Basic Works.* Translated by Rhys Roberts, 1318–1451.

Balakian, Anna Elizabeth. *Literary Origins of Surrealism.* New York: King's Crown Press, 1947.

Baldwin, Charles Sears. *Ancient Rhetoric and Poetic.* New York: Macmillan 1924.

――――. *Medieval Rhetoric and Poetic.* New York: Macmillan 1928.

Bate, Walter Jackson. "Introduction." In *Criticism: The Major Texts,* edited by W. J. Bate, New York: Harcourt Brace Jovanovich, 1970.

Bayer, Raymond. *L'esthétique de la grâce.* 2 vols. Paris: Librairie Felix Alcan, 1933.

Beiswanger, George. "Doing and Viewing Dances: A Perspective for the Practice of Criticism." *Dance Perspectives* 55 (Autumn 1973):8–13.

Bittle, Celestine. *Reality and the Mind*. New York: Bruce Publishing Company, 1936.

Boas, George. "Problems of Literary Evaluation," *The Yearbook of Comparative Criticism* Edited by Joseph Strelka. Pennsylvania State University Press, 1969.

Bové, Paul. "Variations on Authority." In *The Language of Criticism and the Sciences of Man. Proceedings of the 1966 Symposium*. Johns Hopkins University Press, 1970.

Brazzel, S. K. *The Clausulae in the Works of Saint Gregory the Great*. Washington, D.C.: The Catholic University of America Press, 1939.

Bullough, Edward. " 'Psychical Distance' as a Factor in Art and Aesthetic Principle." In *Aesthetics: Lectures and Essays by Edward Bullough*, edited by Elizabeth Wilkinson, 99–130. Stanford, Calif: Stanford University Press, 1957.

Bouhours, Dominique. *Les entretiens d'Ariste et d'Eugène*. Paris: Gabriel Huart, 1691.

Cain, William. *The Crisis in Criticism*. Baltimore: The Johns Hopkins University Press, 1984.

Carrouges, Michel. *André Bréton et les données fondamentales du surréalisme*. Sixième édition. Nrf. Gallimard, 1950.

Chafe, W. L. "Language." In *The New Catholic Encyclopedia*, 8: 367–73. New York: McGraw Hill, 1966.

Chaucer, Geoffrey. "The Nun's Priest's Tale." In *The Works of Geoffrey Chaucer*, edited by F. N. Robinson, 199–205. Boston: Houghton Mifflin Company, 1961.

Cicero. *De Oratore*. Loeb Classical Library, 1942.

———. *Orator*. Loeb Classical Library, 1939.

Clark, A. C. *The Cursus in Medieval and Vulgar Latin*. Oxford: Oxford University Press, 1910.

Clark, D. L. *Renaissance Literary Theory and Practice*. New York: Columbia University Press, 1922.

Coleridge, Samuel Taylor. *Biographia Literaria*. In *Critical Theory since Plato*, edited by Hazard Adams, 468–71. New York: Harcourt Brace Jovanovich Incorporated, 1971.

———. *Coleridge's Lectures on Shakespeare*. Edited by Ernest Rhys. New York: E. P. Dutton, 1907.

Culler, Jonathan. *On Deconstruction*. Ithaca: Cornell University Press, 1982.

Daiches, David. "Imagism." In *Dictionary of World Literature*, edited by Joseph T. Shipley. New York: The Philosophical Library, 1943.

Demetrius. *On Style*. Translated by William Rhys Roberts. Cambridge: The University Press, 1902.

Dennis, John. "The Advancement and Reformation of Modern Poetry." In Adams, *Critical Theory*, 273–76. *Crit. Th. . . . Plato*.

De Saussure, Ferdinand. *Cours de linguistique générale*. Paris: Payot et Cie, 1922.

Dostoevsky, Teodor. *The Idiot*. New York: Dutton, 1934.

Dryden, John. "Original and Progress of Satire." In *Essays of John Dryden*, edited by W. P. Ker. Oxford: at the Clarendon Press, 1900.

Eagleton, Terry. *Literary Theory*. Oxford: Basil Blackwell, 1983.

Eliot, T. S. "Tradition and the Individual Talent." In *Twentieth Century Criticism*, edited by William J. Handy and Max Westbrook. New York: The Free Press, 1974.

Freud, Sigmund. "Creative Writers and Daydreaming." In Adams, *Critical Theory*, 749–53.

Frye, Northrop. "Contexts of Literary Evaluation." In Strelka, *Problems*, 14–21.

Ghiselin, Brewster. "The Light and the Crystal." *Sewanee Review* 67 (1959): 131–35.

Godzich, Wlad. "The Deconstruction of Derrida." In *The Language of Criticism and the Sciences of Man. Proceedings of the 1966 Symposium.* Johns Hopkins University, 1970.

Grant, Elliot, ed. *French Poetry of the Nineteenth Century.* New York: Heath and Company, 1956.

Granville-Barker, H. *Prefaces to Shakespeare.* Princeton: Princeton University Press, 1963.

Hardy, Thomas. *The Complete Poems of Thomas Hardy.* Edited by James Gibson. New York: Macmillan Publishing Co., 1976.

Hausman, C., H. W. Johnstone, C. G. Vaught. "To the Reader." *The Journal of Speculative Philosophy.* University Park: Pennsylvania State University Press, 1987.

Hirsch, Jr., Eric Donald. "Privileged Criteria in Literary Evaluation." In Strelka, *Problems.*

Homer. *The Iliad of Homer.* Translated by Alexander Pope. Printed by W. Boyer for Bernard Lintot between the Temple-Gates, 1715.

———. *The Odyssey of Homer. London: Printed for Bernard Lintot, 1725.*

Horace. *Ars Poetica.* In *Satires and Epistles*, edited by J. B. Greenough. Boston: Ginn and Company, 1890.

Hume, David. *A Treatise of Human Nature.* New York: E. P. Dutton and Company, 1939.

———. "Of the Standard of Taste." In Adams, *Critical Theory.*

Ingarden, Roman. *The Cognition of the Literary Work.* Evanston, Il.: Northwestern University Press, 1973.

———. *The Literary Work of Art.* Evanston, Il.: Northwestern University Press, 1973.

———. *Selected Papers in Aesthetics.* Washington, D.C.: The Catholic University of America Press, 1985.

Jaeger, Werner. *Paideia.* Vol. 3. New York: Oxford University Press, 1944.

James, Henry. "Preface to *The American.*" In *The Art of the Novel*, edited by R. P. Blackmur. New York: Charles Scribner's Sons, 1953.

———. "Preface to *The Aspern Papers.*" In Blackmur, *Art of the Novel.*

———. "Preface to *The Lesson of the Master.*" In Blackmur, *Art of Novel.*

———. "Preface to *The Portrait of a Lady.*" In Blackmur, *Art of the Novel.*

———. "Preface to *The Spoils of Poynton.*" In Blackmur, *Art of the Novel.*

Johnson, Samuel. *The Complete Works of Samuel Johnson.* 12 Vols. Edited by Arthur Murphy. London: J. Nichols and Son, 1810.

———. "Pope" In Murphy, *The Complete Works.* Vol. 2. *The Works of S. Johnson.* Ed. Murphy, Vol. II.

Kant, Immanuel. *Critique of Judgment.* In Adams, *Critical Theory,* 379–99.

Klaeber, Friedrich, ed. *Beowulf and the Fight at Finnsburg.* Boston: Heath, 1950.

La Drière, J. Craig. "Comparative Method in the Study of Prosody." In *Comparative Literature. Proceedings of the ICLA Congress.* edited by W. P. Friedrich. Chapel Hill: University of North Carolina Press, 1949.

———. "Classification." In *Dictionary of World Literature.* Edited by Joseph T. Shipley. Totowa, N. J.: Littlefield Adams and Company, 1968.

———. "Form." *DWL.*

———. "Literary Form and Form in the Other Arts." In *Stil- und Formprobleme in der Literatur.* Edited by P. Böckmann. Heidelberg: C. Winter 1959.

———. "Organic Form." In Shipley, *Dictionary.*

———. "Poetry and Prose." In Shipley, *Dictionary.*

———. "Prosody." In Shipley, *Dictionary.*

———. "Rhetoric and Poetic." In Shipley, *Dictionary.*

———. "Scientific Method in Criticism." In Shipley, *Dictionary,* 1968 and 1972 eds.

———. "Voice and Address." In Shipley, *Dictionary.*

Laird, John. *The Idea of Value.* Cambridge: Cambridge University Press, 1929.

Landor, Walter Savage. "Pericles and Aspasia." In *The Works of Walter Savage Landor.* Vol. 1., edited by T. E. Welby. London: Chapman and Hall, 1927.

Langer, Susanne. *Feeling and Form.* New York: Charles Scribner's Sons, 1953.

Le Grand, Philippe-Ernst. *Etude sur Théocrite.* Paris: Ancienne Librairie Thorin et Fils, 1898.

Lonergan, Bernard *Insight.* New York: The Philosophical Library, 1970.

Longinus. *On the Sublime.* 2d ed. Edited and Translated by William Rhys Roberts. Cambridge: at the University Press, 1907.

Lord, Alfred. *Singer of Tales.* Cambridge: Harvard University Press, 1960.

Lyotard, Jean-François. *The Postmodern Condition.* Minneapolis: University of Minnesota Press, 1979.

Meyer, Leonard B. "Meaning in Music and Information Theory." *Journal of Aesthetics and Art Criticism,* 15 (June 1957): 412–24.

Miall, David S. "Aesthetic Unity and the Role of the Brain." *Journal of Aesthetics and Art Criticism* 35 (Fall 1976): 57–67.

Monk, Samuel Holt. "A Grace beyond the Reach of Art." *Journal of the History of Ideas* 5, no. 2 (April 1944): 131–50.

Osborne, Harold. *Aesthetics and Criticism.* New York: The Philosophical Library, 1955.

Ozenfant, Amédée. Appendix to *Painting and Reality,* by Etienne Gilson. Bollingen Series 35.4. New York: Pantheon Books, 1957.

Plato. *The Dialogues of Plato.* Edited by Edith Hamilton and Huntington Cairns. New York: Bollingen Foundation, 1961.

Pseudo-Plato. *Minos*. Loeb Classical Library, 1927.

Pope, Alexander. "Essay on Criticism." In *The Works of Alexander Pope*. 10 vols. Elwin-Courthope Edition. London: John Murray, 1871.

――――. *Essay on Homer's Battels*. In *The Prose Works of Alexander Pope*. Vol. 1., edited by Norman Ault. Oxford: Shakespeare Head Press, 1936.

――――. "Postscript." In *The Odyssey of Homer*. London: Printed for Bernard Lintot, 1725.

――――. "Preface to the *Iliad*." In Ault, *The Prose Works*.

――――. *Mr. Pope's Preface*. The Works of Shakespeare in Six Volumes. Vol. 1. Edited by Hammer. Oxford: Printed at the Theater, 1744.

Quintilian. *Institutio Oratoria*. 3 vols. Loeb Classical Library, 1921.

Rader, Melvin. "The Artist as Outsider." *Journal of Aesthetics and Art Criticism* 16 (March 1958): 306–18.

Ray, William. *Literary Meaning*. Oxfordshire: Basil Blackwell, 1984.

Rimbaud. Letter to Demény, 5 May 1871. Quoted by Elliott Grant in *French Poetry of the Nineteenth Century*. New York: Heath and Company, 1956.

Root, Robert Kilburn. *The Poetical Career of Alexander Pope*. Princeton: Princeton University Press, 1941.

Sandys, John Edwin. *A History of Classical Scholarship*. Cambridge: University Press, 1921.

Scholes, Robert. *Textual Power*. New Haven: Yale University Press, 1985.

Schrecker, Paul. *Work and History*. Princeton: Princeton University Press, 1948.

Shakespeare, William. *As You Like It*. In *The Complete Works of Shakespeare*. New York: P.F. Collier and Son, 251–80.

――――. *Hamlet*. In *The Complete Works*, 1127–70.

――――. *Macbeth*. In *The Complete Works*, 1100–1120.

――――. *A Midsummer Night's Dream*. In The Complete Works, 167–90.

Slattery, S. M. F. "Beauty in Aesthetics." In *The New Catholic Encyclopedia*. Vol. 2, 207–208.

――――. *Hazard, Form and Value*. Detroit, Mich.: Wayne State University Press, 1971.

――――. "Henry James' Theory of Literary Invention." In *The Grayfriar Lectures*. 2d ser. Loudonville, New York, 1959.

――――. "Looking Again at Susanne Langer's Expressionism." *British Journal of Aesthetics* 27, no. 3 (1987): 247–58.

――――. The Pursuit of Grace in the Technique of the Poetic Process according to Alexander Pope." Ph.D. diss., The Catholic University of America, 1952.

――――. "What Is Literary Realism?" *Journal of Aesthetics and Art Criticism* 21 (1972): 55–62.

Spivak, Gayatri Chakravorty. Preface to *Of Grammatology*, by Jacques Derrida. Translated by Spivak. Baltimore: The Johns Hopkins University Press, 1976.

Sprinker, Michael. *The Yale Critics: Deconstruction in America*: Minneapolis: University of Minnesota Press, 1983.

Stauffer, Donald. *The Golden Nightingale*. New York: Macmillan Company, 1949.

Strelka, Joseph. "Foreword." *Problems of Literary Evaluation*. Edited by Strelka. Penn State University Press, University Park, Pa., 1969.

Sullivan, S. R. *A Study of the Cursus in the Literary Works of Saint Thomas More.* Washington, D.C.: Catholic University of America Press, 1943.

Sweeney, J. L. "Symbolism." In Shipley, *Dictionary,* 1972 ed.

Wellek, René. "Analysis of the Literary Work of Art." In *The Theory of Literature,* by Wellek and Austin Warren. New York: Harcourt Brace and Company, 1949.

Wing-tsit-Chan. "Expressionism." In *Encyclopedia of the Arts,* edited by Dagobert Runes and Henry Schrickel. New York: The Philosophical Library, 1946.

Winters, Yvor. *The Anatomy of Nonsense.* Norfolk, Conn.: New Directions, 1942.

Wordsworth, William. "Preface." *Lyrical Ballads.* 2d ed. In Adams, *Critical Theory,* 432–43.

Young, Edward. "Conjectures on Original Composition." In Adams, *Critical Theory,* 338–47.

Zink, Sidney. "Poetry." In Runes and Schrickel, *An Encyclopedia of the Arts.*

Index